PUT AN EGG ON IT

PUT AN egg ON IT

70 DELICIOUS DISHES *that* DESERVE *a* SUNNY TOPPING

LARA FERRONI

SASQUATCH BOOKS
SEATTLE

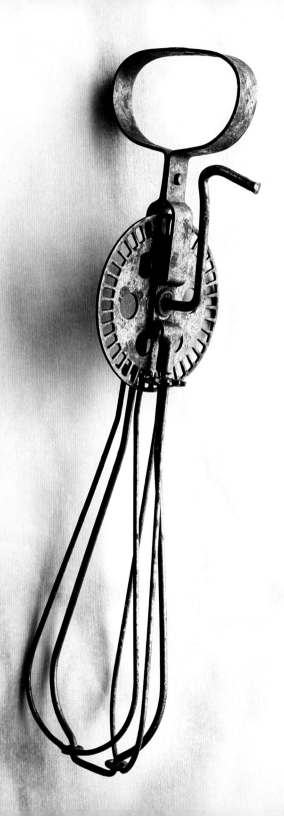

Printed in China

Published by Sasquatch Books
17 16 15 14 13   9 8 7 6 5 4 3 2 1

Editor: Susan Roxborough
Project editor: Michelle Hope Anderson
Design: Anna Goldstein
Photographs: Lara Ferroni

Library of Congress Cataloging-in-Publication
Data is available.
ISBN: 978-1-57061-879-6

Sasquatch Books
1904 Third Avenue, Suite 710
Seattle, WA 98101
(206) 467-4300
www.sasquatchbooks.com
custserv@sasquatchbooks.com

CONTENTS

RECIPE LIST

lunches

mains

sweets

cocktails

ACKNOWLEDGMENTS

Thanks to all chefs who crown dishes with eggs, especially Sunshine Tavern, Fried Egg I'm in Love, Sitka & Spruce, and Wafu. It makes me hungry to even think about your deliciously sunny dishes.

Thanks to Cameron for the great title suggestion, which brought clarity to my egg book vision. There was a pony in there.

Thanks to Maura Greenblum for her tireless recipe testing and all the honest feedback. I hope that you still love to eat eggs after so many recipes in such a short time!

Thanks to Nicole Rejwan for her wonderful assistance in the cover photo shoot. It was always a joy to have you in the studio!

Thanks to Phoenix's egg farm for humanely raising chickens and making such delicious eggs available at my local market.

Thanks to Susan, Michelle, Anna, Christy, and the gang at Sasquatch for helping me share my love of eggs with everyone.

INTRODUCTION

It never fails. When I look at a menu, my eyes magically zoom to any dish where an egg appears. You might, if you listen closely, even hear a little "oooo" escape my lips. (OK, maybe you don't have to listen that closely.)

This love of mine started with New Mexican–style enchiladas. If you don't have family from New Mexico, you might think an enchilada is a rolled tortilla doused in cheese and salsa and baked into almost a casserole. Not that there's anything wrong with that. It's just not what I call enchiladas. In New Mexico, enchiladas are fresh corn tortillas very lightly fried, then dunked into hot red or green chile sauce and placed flat, not rolled, on a plate. Toppings are usually as simple as freshly grated cheese and chopped onion, with another fried and dipped tortilla on top, continuing a few times to create a pancake-like stack of chile-soaked goodness. The whole thing is heated very briefly to melt the cheese, and then—this is the most important part—a perfectly fried sunny-side up egg is placed on top. As you slice, the egg spills into the chile, creating a luscious, gooey mix. It's one of my favorite combinations, and it's just not the same without the egg.

Still, it was many years before I thought adding an egg to sandwiches or pizza was a good idea. I don't quite remember what prompted it, but I do recall vividly that I was sitting in a plaza in Rome when I finally decided I should try an egg on a pizza and discovered what I'd been missing all those years. Just like the enchiladas, the egg added a whole new level of yum. That moment must have flipped some hidden switch in me, because from then on, I became a complete egg fanatic. Fried egg tacos? Yep. Grilled cheese and egg? You betcha. Fried rice crowned with a sunny-side egg? Can you add another?

Now a hot bowl of soup with an egg lightly submerged brings a smile to my face. My eyes light up when cocktail menus include flips and fizzes with floating egg foams. Even desserts seem to shine just a bit more when topped with a billow of meringue.

And so, after years of gushing to my friends and family about my love of an egg on top, jotting down little notes about things that would be even better with eggs, and snapping quick photos on my phone of inspiring eggy dishes at my favorite restaurants, *Put an Egg on It* was born. These seventy egg-inspired dishes—some fancy-pants and some about as lowbrow as you can get without deep-frying Twinkies—are some of my favorites.

EGG BASICS

---

get eggducated

how to pick an egg

As much as my apartment balcony may be a great place to urban-farm, I'm pretty sure my landlord (and neighbors, and husband) wouldn't be happy if I extended that idea to include chickens. The best I can do is to get my eggs at the farmers' market. There I can actually talk to the farmer who raised the chickens (and even go see them at the farm!). I'm blessed to live in Portland, where my local Saturday market has many egg vendors, including those that sell duck eggs and even quail eggs. If that's not an option for you, you'll have to brave the grocery aisle.

I've been known to stand in the grocery store for many minutes staring at the egg display. It's frustrating; some eggs are free-range but come from hundreds of miles away; some are local, but there's no indication of how the birds were raised. How do you choose?

If possible, I try to buy local, pasture-raised, organic eggs. If I have to compromise, I'll get local, pasture-raised, nonorganic ones, as many times the lack of organic status is more bureaucratic than anything. Local farmers humanely raising their chickens aren't likely pumping them full of nasty chemicals. If I can't find local eggs, then I try to find the closest I can that are still humanely raised. However, don't put too much faith in claims like "natural"—or even, unfortunately, "cage-free." Those terms don't necessarily mean happy chickens.

Brown, white, or blue? It really doesn't matter! The eggs will all taste the same and have the same nutritional content if the chickens are raised in the same conditions. If the same brand offers both white and brown, there's really no reason to spend the extra money on the brown.

EGG SIZE

Eggs are sized by weight. A large chicken egg weighs approximately 2 ounces, with 2 tablespoons white and 1 tablespoon yolk. However, eggs are typically not individually measured, but weighed per dozen, so there may be some size variance in any particular batch. A small difference in egg weight won't make much difference in most of your cooking, but for the most consistent baking results, you may want to weigh your eggs.

On the large end, jumbo eggs weigh approximately 2.5 ounces each (30 ounces per dozen). Medium eggs (I've never seen small eggs in a store) are typically the smallest, about 1.75 ounces per egg (21 ounces per dozen). Most recipes are just fine if you use a different-size egg, but if they call for three or more, you'll need to make adjustments: use two jumbo or four medium eggs in place of three large ones. All the recipes in this book assume using large eggs, unless otherwise specified.

Typical duck eggs sold at stores are just a little larger than jumbo eggs, so feel free to substitute a jumbo chicken egg in recipes that call for duck eggs. However, since duck eggs are slightly higher in fat and protein, it's best to use very fresh, free-range chicken eggs in their place.

There's no great chicken egg substitute for quail eggs, since typically you'll use them when only a teeny-tiny egg will do. Quail eggs usually weigh about ½ ounce. However, if you do need to substitute a chicken egg, start with the smallest eggs you can find and drain off some of the white by placing the whole egg in a slotted spoon.

The grade of the egg, either AA, A, or B, is not an indication of size, but rather of exterior and interior quality. Inspectors judge the shell by cleanliness, texture, shape, and strength, and examine the interior by backlighting, which shows the size of the air pocket (smaller in higher-quality eggs) and the distinctness of the yolk.

EGG FRESHNESS

Most eggs you purchase in the store are stamped with a date, but the meaning of that date can vary. USDA eggs are stamped with the date on which the eggs were packed (known as the Julian date, a three-digit code for the day of the year: 001 for January 1, 365 for December 31). This is the date the eggs were washed, graded, and put in the carton, not when they were laid and collected. Non-USDA-graded eggs will be labeled as required by the state, typically also with the Julian date.

Egg cartons may also have a "purchase-by" or "use-by" date. The purchase-by date on USDA eggs must be no more than thirty days after the pack date, while the use-by date must be no more than forty-five days after the pack date. Whether or not your eggs have an expiration date, it's a good idea to use them within three weeks of the Julian date.

As an egg ages, its air pocket can grow, so you can try floating an egg in a glass of salted water to test its freshness (older eggs will float). However, since air pockets can vary by egg grade and not just egg age, this test isn't foolproof. The best test is to crack the egg: a slightly cloudy white is a sign the egg is very fresh. A clear egg white is an indication the egg is aging. Easily broken or flat yolks are a sign of older eggs (or of poor nutrition in the hens). They should still be fine to eat but are best used in scrambles or in baking.

EGG SAFETY

The risk of getting a foodborne illness from eggs is quite low, but it does happen. It's almost impossible for anyone to eat a rotten egg; if you opened one that was bad, you'd know it immediately by its smell.

However, eggs' moisture and nutrient richness make them a tasty breeding ground for bacteria, so safe handling is important. The bacteria of greatest concern is salmonella, which is found inside about 1 in 20,000 eggs (although it's more prevalent on eggshells). Refrigerating eggs prevents the bacteria from growing, and cooking them kills the bacteria. But in the very rare case of contamination, or eating undercooked or raw eggs, salmonellosis can occur—and it's pretty icky. Abdominal cramps, nausea, fever, and other symptoms can start as early as six hours after consuming contaminated food and last for a couple of days. Although salmonellosis is rarely fatal, serious complications can occur in those with delicate or compromised immune systems. And salmonella isn't the only thing to worry about: eggs can also be infected with other disease organisms, including campylobacter, listeria, yeasts, and molds.

So really, why take chances? Unless of course you're jonesing for Steak Tartare, as sometimes we all do (see the recipe on page 48). If you're willing to roll the dice and eat an undercooked or raw egg, these tips will minimize (but not eliminate!) your risk of getting sick:

» Refrigerate your eggs to prevent bacterial growth.

» Throw away any cracked eggs, even if the crack is small.

» Avoid eggs from large-scale industrial producers that keep chickens in unsanitary conditions. Sick chickens are more likely to have sick eggs.

REFRIGERATE OR NOT?

Commercially produced U.S. eggs are required to undergo a power-washing process to remove bacteria—which, ironically, can potentially weaken the porous shells and *introduce* bacteria. Therefore, although most of the world doesn't refrigerate their eggs, it's necessary to refrigerate eggs in North America.

If you buy your eggs directly from a farm and they aren't power-washed, you may be able to store them at room temperature. Ask the farmer what he or she recommends. However, be aware that unwashed eggs may have more bacteria on the shell than those that have been washed. You can give them a bath yourself in warm (not hot) water and a mild, unscented soap. Rinse them in cold water and store them in a clean container (not the same one the unwashed eggs came in).

Cooked eggs should be eaten immediately or be kept refrigerated. Never leave cooked (in the shell or out) eggs out at room temperature for more than an hour.

how to cook an egg

CRACKING

The best way I've found to crack an egg is to hold it by the ends (thumb on the wider end, index finger on the pointy end) and firmly but carefully bang it straight down on a flat surface. The egg will remain intact but have a significant dent. Then use two thumbs to pull the dent apart: the egg should fall right out without any bits of shell falling along with it. Some folks like the one-handed technique. Other than looking a bit fancy, there's not a whole lot of benefit to it, and I've found you're far more likely to get flecks of shell in your bowl.

To separate the white from the yolk, follow the same steps, but instead of letting the egg fall straight into your bowl, tilt it to the side and let the white ooze out over the top, then move it from shell to shell until most of the white is in the bowl. Don't get too greedy—it's better to keep a bit of egg white with the yolk than to accidentally puncture your egg yolk. If you aren't cooking your whites, it's better to go ahead and pour them out into your (very clean) hands, letting them fall through your fingers. While this is messier, it minimizes the chance of getting any bacteria from the outside of the shell.

Another egg-separating tip: I always separate my eggs one at a time into small ramekins: yolks in one, white in the other. Then I dump, one at a time, the individual and yolk-free white into the bowl with the other whites. That way, if the last yolk breaks, I don't end up having to throw out the entire batch of whites!

« soft-boiled

« medium-boiled

« hard-boiled

If you want to get really fancy, try this egg-separating technique that made the rounds on YouTube: hold a small cleaned and dried water bottle with its neck over the yolk of a whole egg, and give it a little squeeze. The yolk will pop right out of the egg white and up into the bottle, where it can be easily squirted out into a separate bowl. Neat!

If you do end up with a bit of shell in the bowl, it's best not to use your fingers to pull it out, particularly out of the whites. You'll get a bit of oil into the egg that can slightly change its ability to whip. And although it's one of the easiest techniques, I don't recommend using another piece of egg shell to retrieve it, unless you're cooking your eggs, lest you introduce shell bacteria. Instead, use a clean spoon to fish it out.

BOILING

There are several different methods for making boiled eggs, but I like steaming them since the eggs are less likely to get jostled around and crack, and are much easier to peel.

Bring a pot of water to a rapid boil over medium-high heat, place your eggs in a vegetable steamer above the water, and cover. Cook 5 minutes for soft-boiled eggs, 8 minutes for medium, and 12 minutes for hard. It's best to peel the eggs immediately to avoid the yolks turning an icky gray color around the edges, so dunk them immediately into an ice bath until they're cool enough to handle.

If you don't have a steamer, try this boiling method: place the eggs in a heavy-bottomed pot and cover them with cold water. Over medium heat, bring the water to a boil. As soon as it boils, turn off the heat, cover the pot, and let the eggs continue to cook to the desired doneness: 5 minutes for soft, 8 minutes for medium, 12 minutes for hard.

Living at high altitude? Since water boils at a much lower temperature up there, your eggs will take a bit longer. Let them sit in the just-boiled water 8 minutes for soft, 12 minutes for medium, and 17 minutes for hard. The higher you are, the longer you'll need to wait. Above 10,000 feet, you'll need to use a pressure cooker to make hard-boiled eggs.

Contrary to what you might think, slightly older eggs are better for boiling than fresh ones; an egg that is three to five days old will peel much more satisfyingly than one just pulled from the chicken's nest, whether boiled or steamed.

Unpeeled hard-boiled eggs can be refrigerated (store them as soon as they have cooled) for up to a week.

FRYING

Use the freshest eggs for frying. Older eggs will have flat yolks that are likely to break while cooking. For the neatest-looking fried eggs, drain off the thinner part of the white by placing the whole egg in a slotted spoon, then place it in a ramekin to pour.

sunny-side up

The most delicious sunny-side up egg I've found is one that follows the French method of slow cooking in butter. Place 1 to 2 tablespoons of butter (or oil if you prefer) in a well-seasoned carbon steel or cast-iron skillet over low heat, and crack your egg onto a saucer. When the butter has just melted (don't brown it!), slide in the egg. Cover the skillet and cook the egg for 5 minutes, until the white has set but the yolk is still runny.

over easy/hard

Follow the same basic method as for sunny-side up eggs—but you'll want to make sure the egg doesn't stick to the bottom of the pan, so that it's easy to flip. You might find it easier to use a non-stick pan. Give the pan a little shake after about 30 seconds to loosen the egg. Once the white closest to the yolk has set, it's time to flip it. If you want to impress someone, learn this method: lift the skillet a little above the burner, handle toward you. Quickly push the pan away from you, and snap up at the same time—the eggs should do a little back roll. A few tries, and you'll get the swing of it.

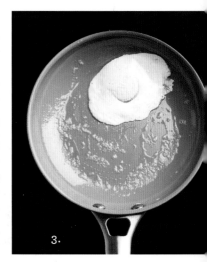

1.

2.

3.

If egg acrobatics aren't your thing, feel free to use a spatula: push it carefully under about three quarters of the egg, then carefully lift slightly, pull toward you, and roll the egg over. Cook for just another 20 seconds for over easy and up to 2 minutes for over hard.

basting

The basting method of frying requires a bit more fat, but also makes what I think are the best-tasting eggs. Plus it gives you the over-easy look without the scary flip.

Place about ¼ inch of oil in a cast-iron skillet, along with 1 tablespoon butter (or lard or duck fat). Heat over medium-high heat until the butter's melted and the oil's just shimmering. Then slide in your eggs. As they cook, use a spoon to push the fat in the pan up on top of the egg white, to help it cook evenly all over. Remove the eggs from the pan when the whites are solid, about 2 to 3 minutes, for a perfectly cooked egg with a runny yolk. For firmer yolks, cook a little longer.

SCRAMBLING

I won't go so far as to say there's a right way to scramble eggs. I grew up eating small-curd and slightly dry egg scrambles, but it seems that most folks out there like larger curds and eggs that are rather moist.

For firmer, drier scrambled eggs, lightly whisk them with a fork, then pour them into a lightly oiled pan (nonstick works best, but a well-seasoned carbon steel pan is also good) over medium-low heat. Keep scrambling them with the fork as they cook until they have set.

For super silky eggs, two tools come in handy: an immersion blender and a rubber spatula. Put your eggs in a tall, wide-mouthed jar and pulse them with the blender until they're very well blended—even a bit foamy. Pour them into a lightly oiled or nonstick pan over medium-low heat. Use the spatula to push the eggs in slow, wide sweeps around the pan's edge until they're set. Use this method for quiches or omelets too.

POACHING

The fresher the eggs, the easier they'll be to poach.

Start by bringing 4 inches of water to a simmer in a pot over medium heat.

Crack an egg into a ramekin, along with a drop of vinegar (which will help the white contract). For the neatest-looking poached eggs, drain off the thinner part of the white by placing the whole egg in a slotted spoon, then return it to the ramekin.

Now grab a whisk with your stirring hand and the ramekin in the other. Whisk the water in a circle to create a bit of a whirlpool and, in as much of a single movement as you can, remove the whisk and drop the egg into the center. The moving water should push the white around the yolk evenly. Don't worry if there are a few stray bits floating about.

Cook for 2 minutes, then use a slotted spoon to gently lift the egg and test for doneness. If you like your poached eggs a little firmer, cook for about 4 minutes total.

Remove the egg from the water with a slotted spoon set it on a paper towel for about 1 minute to drain before serving. If you're making several eggs, make them all up to this point, then reheat them in a pot of warm water for a minute before redraining and serving.

1.

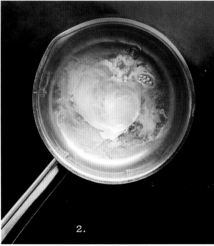

2.

3.

BAKING AND CODDLING

For simple, baked eggs, preheat the oven to 400 degrees F and place ramekins (one per egg), with a bit of butter or oil in the bottom of each, on a baking sheet in the oven for about 3 minutes to warm. Remove the sheet from the oven, add an egg to each ramekin, and bake for about 12 minutes, or until the whites are fully set.

Another technique, coddling, is similar to baking, but instead of putting the eggs in buttered ramekins on a baking sheet, cool and empty ramekins are placed in a heated water bath and baked for about 15 minutes. This approach cooks the egg more evenly, so the whites will be a bit creamier even when fully set.

Both are delicious and easy!

PICKLING

Pickling adds huge flavor to boiled eggs used in salads. To pickle eggs, start by hard-boiling them. You want to make sure they're completely hard throughout, so don't shortcut the time. Let the eggs cool completely and peel them.

There are many different brines in which to pickle your eggs. The most basic is a combination of vinegar, water, and salt. Once you've got the basics down, start adding aromatics and spices for flavor. Dill, mustard seeds, and whole garlic cloves are a great combination. Curry powder and cumin are also great choices, or try star anise, green onion, ginger, and soy sauce. A wedge or two of red beet immersed in the brine will create the most gorgeous jewel-toned eggs.

Pickled eggs should always be stored in the refrigerator, and any leftover brine should be discarded after 3 months.

basic pickled eggs

Makes 1½ to 2 cups of brine, enough for about 4 eggs at a time.

½ cup distilled white vinegar

¼ cup apple cider vinegar

¾ cup water

1 tablespoon salt

» Add all of the ingredients to a heavy-bottomed, nonreactive pot and simmer over medium-low heat for 5 minutes. Pour the brine over peeled eggs in a sterilized jar. Immediately refrigerate. The eggs will be lightly pickled after about an hour, but will taste best the next day. While you can safely store the eggs for weeks, the yolk texture will change, so just pickle what you need at the time and keep the leftover brine in the fridge for the next time you need some pickled eggs.

basic sweet pickled eggs

½ cup distilled white vinegar

¼ cup apple cider vinegar

¾ cup water

⅓ cup sugar

1 tablespoon salt

» For a sweeter pickled egg, make a brine that includes some sugar.

» Prepare as you would Basic Pickled Eggs above.

FLUFFING

The simplest meringue can be made from superfine sugar and egg whites, at a ratio of ¼ cup (50 grams) sugar per egg white. There are two tricks for making a good meringue:

» Use a copper or stainless-steel mixing bowl, if possible, and make sure it's very clean: wipe it down with a cut lemon and dry it with a clean cloth. (If a little bit of oil is hiding in the bowl, your egg whites won't get as fluffy.)

» Room-temperature egg whites will also make a better meringue. To quickly bring refrigerated eggs to room temperature, let them sit in warm (not hot) water for 5 minutes, then separate them, being sure not to get any yolk in the whites.

Here's a sample recipe, using three whites and ¾ cup sugar. You can use it to make any amount of meringue, as long as you keep the ratio of ¼ cup sugar per white.

basic meringue

Makes about 3 cups meringue

3 egg whites, at room temperature
Tiny pinch of salt or cream of tartar
¾ cup sugar

» Whisk the egg whites in a very clean bowl until they're just a bit foamy, then sprinkle in the salt (it will help the whites hold their form). Beat the whites with a whisk or the whisk attachment on a mixer until soft peaks form, about 3 minutes. Sprinkle in the sugar, one large spoonful at a time, until you've added it all. Continue to beat for another 3 minutes, until the meringue is thick, stiff, and glossy; it's now ready to use.

italian meringue

Makes about 3 cups meringue

3 egg whites, at room temperature
Tiny pinch of salt or cream of tartar
¾ cup sugar

» If you're concerned about the raw egg whites in this Basic Meringue recipe above, you can make this Italian meringue, which uses a hot sugar syrup that cooks the eggs.

» Heat the sugar and 3 tablespoons of water over low heat until the sugar melts and reaches 240 degrees F.

» Whisk the egg whites in a very clean bowl until they're just a bit foamy, then sprinkle in the salt (it will help the whites hold their form). Beat the whites with a whisk or the whisk attachment on a mixer until soft peaks form, about 3 minutes. Then slowly pour the hot sugar syrup into the egg white as you continue to beat for another 3 minutes, until the meringue is cold.

BREAKFASTS

don't keep your eggs
all on one biscuit

the breakfast bowl

Most days, if I can't be eating my breakfast within about 10 minutes of opening the refrigerator, I'm skipping it. It's all too easy to reach for something sugary, but for me, that means I'll be hungry all day. It's protein I need, and eggs are the perfect choice. But who wants to eat the same eggs every day? Instead, I grab whatever's in the fridge, sauté it, and top it with an egg or two—all made in the same skillet! Here are some of my favorite Breakfast Bowl variations.

Makes 1 hearty breakfast

» Fry 1 or 2 eggs to your liking, then transfer them to a plate while you quickly whip up one of the ingredient combinations.

1 cup stemmed and sliced kale and 2 or 3 sliced radishes, lightly sautéed

½ (15-ounce) can cannellini beans and 1 or 2 tablespoons harissa, lightly sautéed

½ zucchini, thinly sliced, and 1 teaspoon fresh thyme leaves, lightly sautéed

½ (15-ounce) can warmed pinto beans, ¼ cup salsa, and 1 teaspoon chopped fresh cilantro

3 or 4 pieces smoked salmon, 1 teaspoon capers, and a slice of red onion

1 Roma tomato, seeded and chopped; 2 or 3 fresh basil leaves; and 1 or 2 slices fresh mozzarella

huevos rancheros

There are many different styles of huevos rancheros, many of which involve bucket loads of cheese. I like my "ranch eggs" a whole lot lighter, as they're served at Barelas Coffee House in Albuquerque, New Mexico: simply eggs and green chiles mingled into a soupy delight and scooped up with freshly made flour tortillas. If you can get your hands on them, use fresh New Mexico Hatch green chiles.

NOTE: This recipe makes about 3 cups of sauce, more than you'll need for your huevos. The sauce freezes well, though, so you may want to make a bigger batch to have on hand whenever you get the craving.

Makes 1 hearty breakfast

½ cup chopped onion

1 tablespoon olive oil

1 clove garlic, minced

1 tablespoon all-purpose flour

½ cup chicken stock, divided

2 cups (16 ounces) canned chopped green chiles

1 Roma tomato, seeded and diced

½ teaspoon ground cumin

Salt and freshly ground pepper

2 eggs

2 flour tortillas, warmed

Sour cream, for serving (optional)

» In a large skillet over low heat, cook the onions in the oil until they soften and become translucent, about 10 minutes (don't rush and brown them!). Stir in the garlic and cook for another minute or so, until it's just beginning to take on color, then add the flour and stir to coat. Cook for about 2 minutes, then add ¼ cup stock, stirring to remove any clumps of flour. Add the remaining stock, chiles, tomato, and cumin. Simmer until the chiles and tomatoes are almost melting, about 10 minutes, adding a bit of water if the sauce thickens too much. Season to taste with salt and pepper.

» While the sauce is simmering, fry the eggs sunny-side up. Pour the sauce into a shallow bowl and top with the eggs. Serve with the tortillas and sour cream on the side.

smoked trout with potato hash and a baked egg

Think of this dish as bacon, potatoes, and eggs, without the grease. The smoked trout contributes a taste similar to bacon, but without all the fat. If you can't find smoked trout and don't feel up to smoking your own, feel free to substitute smoked salmon.

Makes 1 hearty breakfast

» Preheat the oven to 350 degrees F.

» Heat the oil in a small ovenproof skillet over low heat. Sauté the onions for about 5 minutes, until they soften. Add the garlic and paprika, and cook for another minute.

» Add the cooked potatoes to the skillet and increase the heat to medium high. Cook until they're a lovely golden brown all over, 5 to 10 minutes, stirring them every now and then. Season to taste with salt and pepper.

» Place the trout on top of the potato mixture and top with the egg. Drizzle with the cream, and bake for 10 minutes, or until the egg has just set. Dust with a bit more paprika, and serve hot in the skillet.

1 tablespoon olive oil

2 tablespoons finely diced onion

1 clove garlic, finely chopped

Pinch of paprika

1 Yukon Gold or other waxy potato, cut into ¼- to ½-inch cubes (I leave the skin on, but you can peel it if you want) and parboiled

Salt and freshly ground pepper

One 2-by-4-inch piece smoked trout

1 egg

2 tablespoons heavy cream

savory oatmeal with a basted egg

Until about a year ago, it never occurred to me that oatmeal could be a savory dish, but once I stumbled upon it (thanks, Penny de los Santos!), it quickly became one of my favorite breakfast (or breakfast-for-dinner) treats. The egg on top mixes up the textures, which could get a little blah by the end of the bowl without it.

Makes 1 hearty breakfast

» In a small saucepan, bring 1½ cups of water with a pinch of salt to a boil and stream in the oats. Reduce the heat to medium-low and simmer until the oats are soft, 30 to 45 minutes. Baste the egg while the oats are cooking.

» Remove the pan from the heat and stir in the olive oil and cheese. Top with the egg and season to taste with salt and pepper. Eat immediately.

½ cup steel-cut (not rolled) oats

1 egg

1 tablespoon olive oil

2 tablespoons shredded Emmentaler or Gruyère cheese

Salt and freshly ground pepper

shakshuka (israeli eggs in peppers and tomatoes)

On one unseasonably warm January morning in Brooklyn, NY, my husband Cam and I chanced by a little gastropub called Lighthouse and realized we were both starving. We sat ourselves at the bar and with a quick scan of the menu knew we'd found something special. As we chatted with the owners (and siblings) Assaf and Naama, we learned how they brought their Israeli culinary roots to New York. I couldn't resist ordering the *shakshuka*—a dish I'd never even heard of before, but knew I'd instantly love. How could I not love eggs poached in a tomato-pepper stew with a name that sounds like some fantastical old-woman dance? One spoonful, and I swore that if I could only eat one dish for the rest of my life, this would be it. Make a double batch, and you can have it for dinner too.

Makes 2 hearty breakfasts

1 teaspoon cumin seeds

2 tablespoons olive oil

½ cup finely chopped onion

3 cloves garlic, smashed and chopped

2 Anaheim peppers, finely chopped

2 serrano peppers, finely chopped

2 teaspoons smoked paprika

2 tablespoons harissa

1 (28-ounce) can crushed tomatoes

Salt and freshly ground pepper

4 eggs

» Heat a large, heavy-bottomed pot over medium-high heat and add the cumin seeds, shaking the pan every once in a while so they toast evenly. When the seeds are quite fragrant, about 1 minute, drizzle the oil into the pot, add the onions, and reduce the heat to medium-low. Cook, stirring occasionally, until the onions are soft and translucent and a bit caramelized, about 5 minutes. Add the garlic and cook for another 2 minutes. Stir in the peppers, paprika, harissa, and the tomatoes with their juice. Increase the heat to medium, and bring the stew to a gentle simmer, cooking until the peppers soften and the juice starts to reduce, about 15 minutes. Season to taste with salt and pepper. Reduce the heat as necessary to keep the stew at a low simmer.

» Remove about half of the stew from the pot and puree in a blender or food processor until smooth. Add the puree back to the pot and cook for another 10 minutes. When the stew is nice and thick and luscious, it's time to cook the eggs.

» In the same pot (or divide the tomato mixture between 2 small pots), create four shallow indentations with a bit of room between them and drop 1 egg into each. Cover the pot and cook for another 4 minutes, or until the eggs are set the way you like them.

» Lighthouse serves this dish with a drizzle of tahini and grilled bread on the side to cut through some of the spice.

savory buckwheat crepes

A simple slice of ham and fresh spinach play well with the eggs in these easy buckwheat crepes. I hope you try other flavor combos as well! The possibilities are endless. Note that the batter needs to sit for an hour, so plan accordingly. You can also make it a day ahead, refrigerate overnight, and bring it to room temperature before cooking. Be sure to whisk the batter to recombine the ingredients before frying the crepes.

I prefer my crepes with the crispy edges you get only when they're straight from the pan, but you can make all the crepes first and keep them in a warm oven while you cook the eggs and ham.

Makes 4 crepes

» In a small bowl, whisk the flour, 1 of the eggs, butter, milk, and salt until you have a smooth batter. Cover and let sit at room temperature for an hour.

» In a large skillet, fry the remaining 4 eggs over easy, then lightly fry the ham. Remove them to a covered plate to keep warm while you make the crepes.

» Heat a small nonstick skillet over medium heat and lightly grease it with oil. Add about 3 tablespoons of batter and swirl to coat the pan. If the batter doesn't spread, add a bit of water to thin it. Cook the crepe for 1 to 2 minutes, or until the edges start to peel away from the sides of the pan. Flip it, and cook for another 30 seconds.

» Place the crepe on a plate and top with a slice of ham, an egg, and ¼ cup spinach. Fold the sides of the crepe in to create a square. Serve immediately, folded side down (or serve open-face, as shown in photo). Repeat with the remaining crepes.

½ cup buckwheat flour

5 eggs

½ tablespoon unsalted butter, melted

½ cup milk

Pinch of salt

4 thin slices of ham

Vegetable oil, for cooking the crepes

1 cup baby spinach leaves

monte cristo with fried eggs, goat cheese, and preserves

French toast and ham together in one sandwich can only be made better by a fried egg! The result is sweet, savory, and creamy all at the same time. Rather than deep-frying, as is often done with the Monte Cristo, I prefer pan-frying in butter to get really nice caramelization on the bread. Note that the sandwich needs to chill for at least an hour before you batter and fry it, or you can make it a day ahead and refrigerate it overnight.

Makes 1 sandwich

2 eggs

2 teaspoons apricot or other preserves, plus more for serving

2 slices rustic country bread

1 slice ham

2 tablespoons goat cheese

2 tablespoons milk

Pinch of ground cinnamon

2 tablespoons butter

Confectioners' sugar, for sprinkling

» Start by frying one of the eggs over easy, being careful not to overcook it.

» Spread 1 teaspoon of preserves on each slice of bread. Top one slice with the ham and then the fried egg, and spread the goat cheese on the other, then place the slice, cheese side down, very gently atop the egg. Wrap the sandwich in plastic wrap and refrigerate for at least 1 hour (and up to overnight).

» In a shallow bowl, whisk together the remaining egg, milk, and cinnamon. Melt the butter in a small skillet over medium heat. Carefully dip each side of the sandwich into the batter and fry for about 2 minutes on each side to caramelize the bread.

» Sprinkle the sandwich with confectioners' sugar and serve to your weirdest food-eating friends with a little extra preserves on the side.

maple syrup–poached eggs and waffles

Wouldn't you love to be one of those fancy people who can plan far enough in advance to make yeasted waffles for breakfast? Me too. That's why, instead, I give you this recipe, which requires only about as much forethought as turning on the waffle iron. And anyway, your waffles will be super fancy because you're serving them with eggs poached in maple syrup. Yep, you read that right: eggs poached in maple syrup.

Makes 2 servings

» Preheat the oven to 250 degrees F and prep your waffle iron according to the manufacturer's instructions.

» In a medium bowl, mix the flour, baking powder, sugar, and salt. In a separate small bowl, whisk together 1 of the eggs and the buttermilk. Pour the egg mixture into the flour mixture and stir just to combine. Then stir in the butter.

» Cook the waffles according to the instructions for your iron, usually about 4 minutes for each, removing them to a cookie sheet in the oven to keep warm. While the waffles are cooking, fry the bacon and set it aside on a paper towel–lined plate to drain.

⅔ cup all-purpose flour

1 teaspoon baking powder

1 teaspoon sugar

Pinch of salt

3 eggs

½ cup buttermilk

3 tablespoons unsalted butter, melted

2 to 4 strips bacon

1 cup Grade A maple syrup, plus more for serving

» When the waffles are done, start the eggs. Place the maple syrup in a small, high-sided saucepan and bring it to a simmer over medium-low heat. Carefully pour 1 of the 2 remaining eggs in (from a ramekin works best), and cook for about 3 minutes, or until the white sets, using a spoon to push some of the syrup over the top of the egg as needed. Gently remove the egg from the pot with a slotted spoon and set it aside. Repeat with the remaining egg.

» To serve, place a waffle on a plate and top with a slice or 2 of bacon, followed by 1 poached egg and a drizzle of maple syrup.

salsa roja chilaquiles

My favorite thing about *chilaquiles*? So much classier-sounding than ordering nachos for breakfast. You should end up with about 2 cups of sauce—more than is needed for this recipe. Extra sauce will keep for weeks refrigerated in a well-sealed container.

Makes 2 hearty breakfasts

» Remove the stems from the chiles and shake out as many of the seeds as you can. (Don't worry if there are still some in there.) Tear the larger chiles into smaller pieces. Dump them all in a bowl and add enough boiling water to cover. Let them sit for at least 20 minutes. Drain the chiles, reserving the soaking water.

» Heat the oil in a large skillet over medium-low heat. Add the garlic, tomato paste, and drained chiles. Cook for about 4 minutes, then add 2 tablespoons of the cilantro, and the epazote. Cook for another 5 minutes, stirring to keep anything from burning.

A variety of dried chiles, roughly 2 to 3 cups, depending on how spicy you like things	½ cup apple cider vinegar
	½ cup honey or agave nectar
Boiling water	Salt
1 tablespoon olive oil	4 eggs
3 cloves garlic, smashed	1 (8- to 10-ounce) bag white corn chips
¼ cup tomato paste	
¼ cup plus 2 tablespoons finely chopped fresh cilantro leaves, divided	¼ cup finely chopped onion
	¼ cup *crumbled cotija* cheese
4 to 5 chopped fresh epazote leaves (optional)	1 tablespoon chopped jalapeño

» Add the chile mixture to a food processor or blender along with the vinegar and honey; puree. If the mixture gets too thick, thin it with a bit of the reserved chile water. (You can also use the chile water as a flavoring for other dishes, such as a pot of pinto beans; it may be very spicy, so use it cautiously.) Taste and add a little salt and a little more vinegar or honey if needed.

» Fry the eggs, sunny-side up. Working in batches, coat the chips in the warm sauce and divide them between 2 plates (or, if you prefer, just make a big platter, nachos-style). Scatter the onion, remaining ¼ cup cilantro, cojita, and jalapeño over the chips and top each with an egg. Drizzle on a bit more chile sauce if desired and serve immediately.

STARTERS

hors d'oeufs and
sunny sides

eggs in a nest (capellini gratin)

I love these soft-cooked quail eggs nestled into crisp and creamy pasta gratin "nests." The edges of the pasta get just a little caramelized and are easy to eat; you can make them in advance and warm them up before adding the eggs. Be sure to serve the nests quickly after the eggs have cooked.

Makes 6 nests

Butter for greasing tin

½ pound spaghetti or capellini

⅓ cup heavy cream

½ cup freshly grated Parmigiano-Reggiano or pecorino cheese, divided

Pinch of freshly ground nutmeg

Pinch of *piment d'espelette* or hot paprika

Sea salt and freshly ground pepper

6 quail eggs

Fresh herbs, fried shallots, or pesto, for garnish

» Preheat the oven to 425 degrees F and lightly butter a regular-size 6-cup muffin tin.

» Cook the pasta according to the package directions until al dente.

» While the pasta is cooking, in a large bowl stir together the cream, ¼ cup of the cheese, nutmeg, and *piment d'espelette*. Season to taste with salt and pepper.

» Using a pasta spoon, scoop the cooked pasta out of the water and into the cream mixture. Stir well to coat each strand. Add a little of the pasta water if the cream starts to clump. Let the pasta rest in the cream for a couple of minutes.

» Using tongs, grab a small amount of the pasta and let it hang for a minute over the bowl to straighten. Then place it in one of the muffin cups, forming a spiral as you lay it in. Don't worry too much about making a perfect nest, but do leave a little indentation in the middle. Repeat with the remaining pasta, filling all the cups. If you still have some cream in the bowl, pour enough into each nest so you can just see it starting to show through the top layer of pasta. If you're out of liquid, get a bit more cream to top off each nest. Divide the remaining ¼ cup cheese among the nests, sprinkling it on top.

» Bake the nests until the tops are golden and bubbly, about 10 minutes. Remove the tin from the oven and carefully, so as not to burn yourself, crack a quail egg into the center of each nest. Reduce the oven temperature to 350 degrees F and bake the eggs for 5 minutes, or until the whites have set.

» Let the gratin cool for 5 to 10 minutes to firm up before serving. Garnish with the herbs, shallots, or a little pesto. Yum!

crostini with poached eggs and creamy mustard kale

Kale may be the ingredient of the moment, but for good reason. Not only is it packed with nutrients, it's also one of the least bitter of the braising greens. This recipe is a little twist on creamed spinach and toast, and makes a great starter. Any kale will do, but I like *cavolo nero* (aka dinosaur kale or Lacinato) because its long, narrow leaves more neatly slice into ribbons. Depending on the size of your bread, quail eggs or medium chicken eggs are likely to work better than large or extra-large here.

Makes 6 crostini

» Place the baguette slices on a baking sheet and broil for 2 to 3 minutes, until the bread browns. Set aside.

» Melt the butter in a large, heavy-bottomed skillet over medium-low heat and add the shallot and garlic, along with a sprinkling of salt and pepper. Cook for about 3 minutes, until the shallots get nice and soft. Add the kale and cook for 6 to 8 minutes, until the kale wilts and softens. Increase the heat to medium-high, add the vermouth, and cook until it's just evaporated, about 1 minute. Add the cream and mustard, stirring until they're completely incorporated. Reduce the heat to medium and cook until the sauce reduces slightly and tightens up around the kale, about 2 minutes. Taste and add a bit more salt and pepper if needed. Reduce the heat to low to keep the mixture warm.

» Poach the eggs, using a slotted spoon to gently lift them from the water. Set them on a paper towel for a moment to drain.

» Top each crostini with a generous scoop of the kale mixture and a poached egg. Serve immediately.

Six 3- to 4-inch-thick slices baguette

2 tablespoons unsalted butter

1 large shallot, thinly sliced (about ⅓ cup)

2 cloves garlic, thinly sliced

Salt and freshly ground pepper

1 bunch kale, stems removed, roughly chopped

¼ cup dry vermouth

½ cup heavy cream

1 tablespoon Dijon mustard

6 quail or medium chicken eggs

scrambled egg cups with pickled red onions

A perfectly scrambled egg topped with crème fraîche and caviar, carefully spooned into a cleaned eggshell, feels particularly indulgent to me—definitely not a dish for every day. But skip the finicky shell and replace the caviar with pickled red onion, and now you've got an indulgence for any day!

Makes 4 egg cups

¼ cup sugar

2 cups apple cider vinegar

1 teaspoon kosher salt

1 red onion, finely chopped

2 teaspoons mustard seeds

5 peppercorns

4 eggs

2 teaspoons crème fraîche

Maldon or other flaked sea salt

» In a medium saucepan over medium-low heat, add the sugar, vinegar, and salt. Simmer until the sugar dissolves. Add the onion, mustard seeds, and peppercorns, and remove the pan from the heat. Let the onions cool in the liquid for about 30 minutes, then pack them into a clean jar with a tight seal. (You'll only need a teaspoon or so each time you use it, and it will keep, refrigerated, for weeks.)

» Scramble the eggs. To serve, divide them among 4 small egg cups or ramekins; top each with ½ teaspoon crème fraîche, ¼ teaspoon of the pickled onions, and a sprinkle of sea salt.

nachos with eggs

There's something about a big pile of cheesy nachos spiked with pickled jalapeños and a couple of dollops of sour cream and guacamole that makes the perfect end to a day of hiking, skiing, or anything that gets your heart pumping. But I've never seen nachos with an egg on them—and that's a travesty I rectify in this recipe.

Makes 1 large plate of nachos

» Preheat the oven to 350 degrees F and line a baking sheet with parchment paper. Spread the chips on the prepared sheet in a single layer and bake for 5 minutes.

» While the chips bake, fry the eggs sunny-side up.

» Sprinkle the chips with the beans, cheese, onion, and tomato. Return the sheet to the oven for 5 minutes until the cheese has melted. Sprinkle with the jalapeños.

» Working from one edge, fold one-third of the chips toward the center, and then fold over again. Transfer the chips to a platter and scatter the cilantro over the top. Top with the eggs, sour cream, and guacamole.

6 cups corn tortilla chips

2 eggs

1 cup whole pinto beans

1 cup shredded Monterey Jack cheese

¼ cup chopped red onion

¼ cup seeded, chopped tomato

¼ cup chopped pickled jalapeños

¼ cup chopped fresh cilantro leaves

2 tablespoons sour cream (optional)

2 tablespoons guacamole (optional)

steak tartare

It wouldn't be an egg book without some sort of government-approved warning about the dangers of consuming raw food, like you find on most restaurant menus these days. A steak tartare recipe seems a suitable place as any to let you know that "consuming raw or undercooked meats, poultry, seafood, shellfish, or eggs may increase your risk of foodborne illness." It's a risk I'll take any day, using high-quality ingredients, in order to treat myself to the occasional steak tartare.

Makes 8 appetizer servings

2 teaspoons capers

2 teaspoons Dijon mustard

1 egg yolk

10 ounces beef tenderloin, cut into small dice, covered, and chilled

1 tablespoon finely chopped red onion

2 tablespoons finely chopped Italian parsley

4 teaspoons olive oil

2 dashes Worcestershire sauce

1 teaspoon sriracha or harissa

½ teaspoon sea salt

½ teaspoon freshly ground pepper

8 quail egg yolks

» In a medium glass or ceramic bowl, mix the capers with the mustard, breaking up the capers slightly. Whisk in the egg yolk with a fork. Add the tenderloin, onion, parsley, oil, Worcestershire, sriracha, salt, and pepper, and fold gently with a rubber spatula to combine well. Cover with plastic wrap and chill for 5 minutes.

» To serve, divide the tartare into 8 equal mounds. Using a spoon, make a small well in the top of each and top with a quail yolk.

roasted eggplant puree with harissa and shaved egg

Roasted eggplant puree, also known as baba ghanoush, may not appear on appetizer tables as often as hummus, but it should. Topped with shaved egg and a healthy spoonful of harissa, it's a delicious smoky, creamy, and quite healthy dip. I like to serve it with pita, crostini, or celery spears and a sprinkle of pomegranate seeds, when in season.

Makes a nice snack for 6 to 8

» Preheat the oven to 375 degrees F and line a baking sheet with parchment paper.

» Peel the eggplant and slice it into large spears. Place the spears and garlic on the prepared sheet. Drizzle with olive oil and sprinkle with sea salt to taste. Roast for 15 minutes, or until the eggplant is completely softened.

» Add the roasted eggplant, lemon juice, and the 2 tablespoons olive oil to a food processor or blender and puree. Season to taste with salt and pepper.

» Transfer the puree to a serving bowl. Use a fine cheese grater to shave the egg onto the puree, then spoon on the harissa.

1 globe eggplant

2 cloves garlic, peeled

2 tablespoons olive oil, plus more for drizzling the eggplant

Sea salt

1 tablespoon lemon juice

Salt and freshly ground pepper

1 hard-boiled egg

1 tablespoon harissa

blasted cauliflower with eggs

Cauliflower undergoes an almost magical transformation when blasted in a hot oven. The florets soften and begin to caramelize, yielding a buttery sweetness. A little mustard and red pepper flakes to your taste add kick, and hard-boiled eggs tie the whole thing together with a surprising, almost creamy mouthfeel that makes it hard to resist another bite.

Makes 4 to 6 side servings

» Preheat the oven to 450 degrees F and line a baking sheet with parchment paper.

» Cut the cauliflower into medium florets and toss them with the oil, red pepper flakes, pine nuts, raisins, mustard, and salt and pepper to taste in a large bowl. Spread them in an even layer on the prepared sheet. Bake until they're golden and caramelized on the edges, about 30 to 45 minutes. Transfer to a bowl.

» Chop the eggs and sprinkle them over the cauliflower along with another drizzle of oil. Serve immediately.

1 head cauliflower

1 tablespoon olive oil, plus more for drizzling

¼ to 1 teaspoon red pepper flakes

¼ cup pine nuts

¼ cup golden raisins

¼ teaspoon dried mustard

Sea salt and freshly ground pepper

2 hard-boiled eggs

israeli couscous with chicken sausage and over-easy eggs

Israeli couscous, also known as *ptitim*, is little pasta balls that are vaguely reminiscent of tapioca pearls, but in a much less goopy way. I love the little spring they have when cooked perfectly al dente and the way they soak up the flavors of the sausage and preserved lemon in this Mediterranean-inspired dish. Preserved lemons can usually be found in the international food aisle of most grocery stores, but if you can't find them, feel free to use fresh lemon zest.

Makes 4 servings

2 tablespoons olive oil

1 cup Israeli couscous

2 links chicken sausage

½ onion, thinly sliced into quarter rounds

2 plum tomatoes, seeded and chopped

1 tablespoon chopped preserved lemon

½ cup dry white wine

1½ cups chicken or vegetable stock

1 tablespoon finely chopped Italian parsley

4 over-easy eggs

» Heat 1 tablespoon of the oil in a large, lidded cast-iron skillet over medium-high heat. When it's shimmering, add the couscous. Stir to coat and toast for 1 minute. Transfer to a bowl and set aside.

» Add the sausage to the skillet and cook for 2 to 3 minutes to brown all sides. Then splash in about ¼ cup of water and cook another 4 to 5 minutes, until the water evaporates and the juice runs clear. Set it aside on a plate.

» Add the onion and remaining oil and cook for 3 minutes, or until softened. Add the tomatoes and the preserved lemon, and cook for about 3 minutes, until the tomatoes are soft. Add the wine and reduce, about 4 minutes. Cut the sausage into ¼-inch-thick slices and add it back to the skillet, with any juices that have collected. Add the couscous and pour in the stock. Bring to a boil, then reduce the heat to medium-low and cover the skillet. Cook for 10 to 12 minutes, until the couscous is tender. Remove the pan from the heat and toss in the parsley.

» Divide the couscous mixture between 4 bowls and top each with an egg.

baked eggs with chickpeas, spinach, anchovy, and tomatoes

The beauty of this one-dish side is that while the eggs cook to the perfect temperature, the chickpeas soften, the spinach wilts, and the cherry tomatoes begin to plump, heightening all the flavors. The anchovy on top adds what I think is the perfect little bite to finish, but is also easy to leave off for your vegetarian friends.

Makes 6 side servings

» Preheat the oven to 350 degrees F.

» Divide the chickpeas among 6 wide, shallow, oven-safe ramekins, followed by a heaping teaspoon of the tomato paste and a splash of olive oil. Stir to coat the chickpeas. Layer on the spinach leaves and 2 cherry tomatoes per ramekin, then top each ramekin with an egg. Bake for about 15 minutes, or until the egg whites are set, but the yolks are still soft.

» To serve, top each egg with an anchovy and pepper to taste.

1 (15-ounce) can chickpeas

3 tablespoons tomato paste

2 tablespoons olive oil

5 ounces baby spinach leaves, well washed

12 to 15 cherry tomatoes, halved

6 eggs

6 white anchovies

Freshly ground pepper

baked mini pumpkin pots

I think "pumpkin pots" might just be one of my new word combinations. Pumpkin pots. Pumpkin pots. Pumpkin pots. It just makes me happy the way the words flow together. It also makes me happy the way the flavors of the pumpkin, sausage, herbs, and eggs come together in this perfect little side dish for fall feasts.

Makes 4 mini pots

4 mini pumpkins (about 1 pound each)

4 ounces sweet or hot bulk sausage

5 eggs

4 pieces stale bread (any nonsweet kind), cut into cubes

1 tablespoon minced fresh sage, or 1 teaspoon dried

1 tablespoon minced Italian parsley

½ teaspoon salt

½ teaspoon freshly ground pepper

4 teaspoons crème fraîche (optional)

» Preheat the oven to 350 degrees F and line a baking sheet with parchment paper. Slice the top quarter off each pumpkin and remove the seeds and stringy bits.

» In a medium skillet over medium-high heat, sauté the sausage for 3 to 4 minutes, until cooked through. Drain off any rendered fat and set aside.

» Whisk 1 of the eggs, and toss it in a large bowl with the sausage, bread cubes, sage, parsley, salt, and pepper until well combined.

» Fill each pumpkin with the stuffing mixture to a little less than 1 inch from the top, and place it on the prepared sheet. Bake for 40 minutes, until the pumpkins have softened. Remove the pan from the oven and use a spoon to compress the stuffing a little. Pour 1 of the remaining 4 eggs into each pumpkin. Lightly cover the pumpkins with a sheet of aluminum foil. Increase the heat to 400 degrees F and return the sheet to the oven. Bake for another 10 minutes, until the eggs are just set.

» Serve hot, topped with about a teaspoon of crème fraîche and more salt and pepper to taste.

brussels sprout hash

If brussels sprouts had been served this way when I was a kid, instead of being little balls of gray, bitter mush, I might not have missed out on twenty-something years of one of my favorite fall vegetables. How sad!

Makes 4 servings

» Heat the oil in a medium, lidded cast-iron skillet over medium heat. When it's shimmering, add the rosemary. Cook for about 1 minute, then remove the sprig, setting it aside on a plate to cool. Add the onion and garlic and reduce the heat to medium-low. Cook until the onion softens, about 5 minutes. Add the sprouts and increase the heat to medium-high. Chop up a bit of the fried rosemary leaves (discarding the woody stem) and add them to the pan. Stirring frequently, cook until the sprouts are golden on the edges, about 5 minutes.

» Use a large spoon to create 4 wells in the sprouts and carefully pour an egg into each. Reduce the heat to medium-low, cover, and cook for 2 to 3 minutes, until the eggs are set.

» To serve, using a large spoon, carefully scoop from under each egg, gathering a bit of the sprout hash as you go. Season with salt and pepper to taste.

2 tablespoons grapeseed or olive oil

1 (5-inch) sprig fresh rosemary

¼ cup chopped onion

2 cloves garlic, minced

4 cups shredded brussels sprouts

4 eggs

Salt and freshly ground pepper

sautéed chard
with sunny-side up eggs

This delicious side dish is often my go-to lunch whenever I find myself staring at an almost empty fridge. I seem to almost always have braising greens and eggs, and I can be eating in less than ten minutes. On days when I want a heartier dish, I add a few pieces of sautéed chicken, a slice of bacon, or even a bit of smoked salmon.

Makes 2 to 4 side servings or 1 hearty lunch

1 tablespoon olive oil

1 bunch chard, stems removed and leaves sliced into thin ribbons

1 clove garlic, minced

Sea salt

2 eggs

Freshly ground pepper

» Heat the oil in a large skillet over medium-high heat. When it's shimmering, add the chard and sprinkle with the garlic and sea salt to taste. Sauté until the chard has softened, about 3 minutes. Transfer it to a bowl.

» Fry the eggs sunny-side up in the same skillet and serve on top of the chard. Season to taste with a bit more sea salt and pepper.

SALADS & SOUPS

---

the nest course

asparagus with pistachios and shredded egg

I tend to get into a real rut with asparagus. It's so delicious simply grilled with a bit of salt and lemon that I forget what a flexible side it makes. Rice vinegar and sesame oil give this salad a subtle Asian flavor, but its sweet nuttiness pairs well with any food.

Makes 4 servings

» In a medium bowl, mix the vinegar, oil, and soy sauce.

» Prepare a medium bowl of ice water, and set aside.

» Bring a medium pot of water to a boil. Snap off the woody ends of the asparagus spears and add to the boiling water for about 30 seconds, until the color brightens. Immediately move the asparagus to the ice water, then drain and add it to the bowl with the dressing. Stir to coat. Use a coarse cheese grater to shred the egg.

» To serve, divide the asparagus among 4 plates. Sprinkle with the pistachios and shredded egg.

3 tablespoons rice vinegar

1 teaspoon sesame oil

1 tablespoon soy sauce

1 bunch asparagus (about 1 pound)

1 hard-boiled egg

¼ cup shelled pistachios or slivered almonds, toasted and chopped

grandma's potato salad with sorrel and eggs

My grandmother's potato salad is something special. It's got the perfect balance of tangy vinegar, a teensy bit of heat from mustard, and the perfect creaminess from just the right amount of mayo. It's not at all sweet, except from a little sweet onion. The potatoes manage to be the perfect combination of soft and firm. The only problem? The eggs get mixed in, so you might not even know they were there. This salad has the same great flavors, but I prettied it up with a bit of sorrel and put some eggs on top so they don't get lost.

Makes 4 servings

8 medium new potatoes

2 tablespoons apple cider vinegar

2 tablespoons mayonnaise

1 teaspoon mustard

2 green onions, chopped

4 medium-boiled eggs, sliced into rounds

Salt and freshly ground pepper

4 cups roughly chopped sorrel or watercress

1 tablespoon olive oil

» Place the whole potatoes in a pot of cold water and bring the water to a boil. Cook for about 8 minutes, or until you can pierce the potatoes with a fork. Drain and set them aside to cool.

» Cut the cooled potatoes into quarters, and toss them in a large bowl with the vinegar, mayonnaise, mustard, green onion and 2 of the eggs. Season to taste with salt and pepper. If you have the time, cover and chill the salad overnight. The flavors will blend and improve.

» Place the sorrel in a bowl and top with the potato mixture. Layer the remaining eggs on top, drizzle with the olive oil, and serve.

crab chipotle cobb salad

Little rows of all the good salad stuff—crab, tomato, bacon, and corn—and a dressing with a "pow" make this salad a great (and filling) lunch for two. If you like your dressing a little more or less spicy, adjust the amount of adobo sauce.

Makes 2 to 4 servings

¼ cup plain yogurt

½ cup buttermilk

1 tablespoon lime juice

1 tablespoon finely chopped red onion, divided

1 tablespoon adobo sauce (from a can of chipotle chiles)

½ cup corn

¼ cup fresh cilantro leaves

1 head butterhead or other lettuce, chopped

½ cup lump crabmeat

1 avocado, peeled, seeded, and chopped

1 plum tomato, seeded and chopped

2 strips cooked bacon, chopped

2 hard-boiled eggs, chopped

» In a small bowl, whisk together the yogurt, buttermilk, lime juice, ½ tablespoon of the red onion, and adobo sauce. Cover and chill.

» In another bowl, mix the corn and cilantro with the remaining ½ tablespoon onion.

» Arrange the lettuce to cover the bottom of a large salad platter. Arrange the corn mixture, crab, avocado, tomato, and bacon in rows on top of the lettuce. Sprinkle with the eggs and drizzle with the chipotle dressing.

baby beets and pickled eggs

Pickled eggs make an unexpected and incredibly flavorful addition to easy roasted beets and onions. This dish is equally great on the dinner table as it is in your picnic basket.

Makes 4 side servings

» Preheat the oven to 375 degrees F and line a baking sheet with parchment paper. Scrub and trim the beets, and halve them. Peel the onion, and cut it into 8 wedges. Scatter the beets and onion on the prepared sheet and drizzle with the olive oil and salt. Roast for about 30 minutes, or until the beets have softened slightly. Cover and chill for 30 minutes.

» To serve, place the beets and onions in a bowl, and top with the egg(s) and tarragon.

10 to 14 (2 pounds) small red or golden beets

1 red onion

1 tablespoon olive oil

½ teaspoon sea salt

1 or 2 Basic Sweet Pickled Eggs (page 16, pickled with 1 to 2 wedges red beet), cut into wedges or rounds

1 teaspoon finely chopped fresh tarragon

farro salad with radicchio and apples

Slightly sweet beet-pickled eggs add some zing to this hearty harvest salad. Be sure not to overcook the farro; the grain should still have a nice bite.

Makes 8 servings

» Add the farro to a small, lidded, heavy-bottomed pot and add enough water to cover by about ½ inch (about 2 cups water). Bring the water to a boil, cover, and reduce the heat to low. Cook until the water is absorbed and the grains have softened but are still al dente, about 25 minutes. Set aside.

» Preheat the oven to 425 degrees F and line a baking sheet with parchment paper. Toss the shallots, apples, and radicchio with 1 tablespoon of the olive oil in a medium bowl and season to taste with salt and pepper. Spread on the prepared sheet. Bake for about 12 minutes, stirring once after 7 minutes, until the apples are golden and soft.

» In a large bowl whisk together the remaining 3 tablespoons olive oil, vinegar, mustard, and honey. Gently stir in the farro, apple mixture, and chives. Taste and add more salt and pepper if needed. Sprinkle the eggs on top.

1½ cups farro

2 large shallots, thinly sliced

2 Golden Delicious apples, cored and diced

1 small head radicchio, cut into wedges

¼ cup olive oil, divided

Salt and freshly ground pepper

3 tablespoons sherry vinegar

1 tablespoon Dijon mustard

1 teaspoon honey

1 teaspoon chopped chives

2 Basic Sweet Pickled Eggs (page 16, pickled with 1 to 2 wedges red beet), chopped

creamy green goddess wedge

Iceberg lettuce doesn't usually elicit oohs and aahs from me. So why is it that the simple wedge slice with an herby drizzle makes such a statement? Instead of typical blue cheese crumbles, this wedge gets its little extra from the grated eggs.

Makes 4 salads

2 tablespoons chopped fresh tarragon leaves

1 clove garlic, chopped

2 tablespoons chopped chives or green onions

2 tablespoons white wine vinegar

1 tablespoon lemon juice

½ cup plain Greek yogurt

2 tablespoons olive oil

Salt and freshly ground pepper

2 hard-boiled eggs

1 head iceberg or butterhead lettuce

» In a food processor or blender puree the tarragon, garlic, and chives with the vinegar, lemon juice, yogurt, and oil. Season to taste with salt and pepper.

» Use a coarse cheese grater to shred the eggs. Cut the lettuce into quarters and place each quarter on a plate. Drizzle on the dressing and sprinkle with the shredded egg.

sopa de ajo (spanish bread soup)

Since so much of this soup's flavor comes from the paprika, be sure to use fine-quality smoked Spanish paprika for this recipe, either hot or sweet.

Makes 4 servings

» Preheat the oven to 350 degrees F. Spread the bread cubes evenly on a baking sheet. Bake for 15 minutes, or until the cubes are golden brown just on the edges. Remove the baking sheet from the oven but leave the oven on.

» Pour the oil into a small soup pot over medium-high heat. Add the toasted bread, and stir to coat. Add the garlic, paprika, and salt. Mix well and cook for 2 or 3 minutes, or until fragrant. Add the stock and bring to a boil. Reduce the heat and let the soup simmer for 5 minutes.

» Ladle the soup into 4 individual ovenproof bowls (I like to use mini coquettes), filling them three-quarters full. Top each with an egg. Bake for about 10 minutes, until the eggs have set.

» Sprinkle with a bit more paprika and salt, and serve hot.

½ loaf (about ½ pound) country bread, cut into 1-inch cubes

2 tablespoons olive oil

6 cloves garlic, chopped

1 teaspoon smoked Spanish paprika

1 teaspoon sea salt

1 quart chicken stock

4 eggs

mayiritsa (greek lamb, egg, and lemon soup)

This soup is traditionally made with lamb intestine, but since that tends to make most people queasy—not to mention that lamb intestines aren't exactly available at most corner markets—this recipe uses easier-to-find lamb parts. Because really, it's the lemon and egg that make this soup a luscious, creamy, and tangy bowl of comfort. Note that this recipe is best made a day ahead.

Makes 8 servings

3½ pounds lamb shoulder

1 large onion, peeled and cut into wedges

2 stalks celery, diced

2 carrots, diced

5 black peppercorns

½ cup (1 stick) butter

1 cup minced green onions

½ cup minced fresh dill

4 eggs

6 tablespoons lemon juice

Salt and freshly ground pepper

» Trim any fat from the lamb shoulder. Place a large Dutch oven over medium-high heat and sear the shoulder on all sides, about 3 minutes per side. Add the onion, celery, carrots, and peppercorns to the pan and cover with water. Bring the water to a boil and then reduce to a simmer, covering slightly. Cook for 2 to 3 hours, until the lamb is very tender.

» Remove the meat from the pot and wrap well. Strain out the vegetables, keeping the broth and discarding the solids; place the liquid in an air-tight container. Refrigerate the meat and broth separately until cold (overnight is best). When the broth has chilled, scrape any hardened fat from the top and discard.

» In a large, heavy-bottomed soup pot, melt the butter. Add the green onions and dill, and cook over low heat for 5 minutes.

» Chop the lamb into small pieces and add them to the pot, along with the broth. Simmer over low heat for 20 minutes to warm.

» In a large bowl, whisk the eggs and stream in the lemon juice. Gradually ladle 2 cups of the hot broth into the egg mixture, then pour this mixture back into the soup pot. The broth will become smooth and creamy, but if you get a few strands of egg white, don't worry. Cook for about 5 more minutes on the lowest heat, season to taste with salt and pepper, and serve.

cream of broccoli soup with grated eggs

Comfort food often comes in the form of heavy cream, gobs of cheese, and pounds of butter—especially when broccoli is involved. This soup is just as comforting without making you feel like you've just eaten a huge bowl of gravy.

Makes 4 servings

1 tablespoon unsalted butter

½ cup chopped yellow onion

1 pound broccoli, finely chopped

½ cup dry white wine

4 cups chicken stock

1½ cups water

¼ cup heavy cream

½ cup buttermilk

Salt and freshly ground pepper

2 hard-boiled eggs

» Melt the butter in a large soup pot over medium heat, then add the onions. Reduce the heat to medium-low and cook until the onions have softened and are translucent, about 10 minutes. Add the broccoli and cook for 5 minutes, or until the broccoli lightly caramelizes.

» Stir in the wine and cook until it is completely reduced, about 10 minutes. Add the stock and water, and bring to a boil. Reduce the heat and simmer for 30 minutes, until the broccoli is completely soft. Add the cream and buttermilk. Take the pan off the heat and, using an immersion blender, pulse a little to break up any large pieces of broccoli. Feel free to puree longer if you prefer a completely smooth soup. Return the pot to the heat, and simmer the soup for another 5 minutes. Season to taste with salt and pepper.

» Use a coarse cheese grater to grate the eggs. Divide the soup among 4 bowls and sprinkle with the grated egg.

LUNCHES

small bites that are
hard to beat

havarti, avocado, serrano, and egg sandwich

There are times when I simply have to do a little happy dance. One of those times was when I found out that the new food cart down the street from my house was going to be something called Fried Egg I'm in Love. The only thing I can't resist more than a meal with an egg on it? Great puns.

This sandwich is inspired by my go-to sandwich at Fried Egg I'm in Love; there, it's called Free-Range Against the Machine, but I call it the perfect lunch. If it's summer, and you can find amazing tomatoes, feel free to add a slice.

Makes 1 sandwich

» Poach the egg and set it aside to drain. Melt the butter over medium-low heat in a skillet large enough to hold the two slices of bread side by side. Place the bread in the skillet and top one slice with the havarti, spinach, and peppers. Toast for about 2 minutes.

» When the bread is golden brown (you can easily check its doneness on the untopped slice), carefully remove the cheese-topped slice from the pan and place it on a plate. Top with the avocado, the egg, and salt and pepper to taste, then gently top with the other slice of bread (no flipping needed!). Devour.

1 egg

1 tablespoon butter

2 slices whole grain bread

1 slice havarti cheese

½ cup fresh spinach

½ serrano pepper, sliced into rings

½ avocado, peeled and sliced

Salt and freshly ground pepper

bbq chicken and egg sandwich

If you're in a bind for time, using a rotisserie chicken from the grocery store is a fine substitute for making your own barbecued chicken. But if you're not in a rush, whip up a batch of this delicious barbecue (which makes extra sauce) and freeze any leftovers in individual servings for a quick bite later in the week.

Makes 6 sandwiches

¼ cup tomato paste

½ cup water

½ cup apple cider

½ cup soy sauce

1 cup distilled white vinegar

¼ cup honey

½ cup minced shallot

⅓ cup minced serrano or jalapeño peppers with seeds

¼ cup minced garlic

Salt

6 boneless chicken thighs

6 eggs

6 small brioche buns

2 slices red onion, separated into rings

» Start by making the sauce. Add the tomato paste to a medium saucepan, with a splash of the water. Stir to thin the paste, then add the remaining water a little at a time. Stir in the apple cider, soy sauce, vinegar, honey, shallot, peppers, and garlic. Bring the mixture to a boil, stirring, then reduce the heat and briskly simmer, stirring occasionally, until sauce is reduced to 2¼ cups, about 1 hour. (Stir frequently toward the end of cooking to prevent sticking.) Taste and add salt if needed. Place about half of the sauce in a large bowl, saving the rest for later use.

» You'll get the most flavor if you grill the chicken. Heat an outdoor grill to medium-high and lightly oil the grill rack. Place the chicken on the grill, skin side down. Cook for about 10 minutes, then flip the chicken and continue to cook until the internal temperature reaches 165 degrees F on a meat thermometer, another 10 to 15 minutes. Remove the chicken from the grill and dip it in the bowl with the sauce, turning to coat. Return the chicken to the grill and cook for another 3 to 4 minutes on each side, until the chicken begins to caramelize.

» If you don't have a grill, you can make the chicken in the oven on a broiler pan. Heat the oven to 450 degrees F and cook the chicken for about 10 minutes on each side, or until the internal temperature reaches 165 degrees F. Coat with the sauce as described above, return the chicken to the oven, and broil for about 4 minutes on each side.

» While the chicken is cooking, prepare the eggs, either over easy or poached.

» To serve, spread a bit of BBQ sauce on each of the bottom buns, and top with a chicken thigh, a ring or two of onion, and an egg.

hot dog with scrambled eggs and hot sauce

I might have gotten a funny look from the bartender at Nick's Famous Coney Island in Portland when I ordered my dog with an egg on it, but she was still more than happy to oblige. That egg was delightfully runny sunny-side up, but while delicious, it was too messy even for me. Scrambled, with plenty of hot sauce, seems to be a better fit for the *je ne sais quoi* of a hot dog.

Makes 1 hot dog

1 hot dog or Polish sausage
1 teaspoon butter
2 eggs, scrambled
1 hot dog bun
Plenty of hot sauce

» You don't really need a recipe for this, but here is one anyway.

» It starts with the perfect way to cook a hot dog without a grill. Heat a skillet that will fit your hot dog over medium-high heat. Add about ¼ cup of water to the skillet and bring it to a rapid boil. If you want to get fancy, you can use a little beer instead. When the water is at a good steam, add the hot dog. Cook until the water is completely gone. Then add the butter to the pan and cook the dog, flipping occasionally, until it's a little caramelized all over, about 3 minutes. While the hot dog is cooking, make your scrambled eggs.

» To serve, nestle the hot dog in its bun and top with the scrambled eggs and many shakes of hot sauce.

croque madame

I thought about doing something to mix up this traditional egg, ham, and cheesy béchamel sandwich, but then I remembered the old record series, Hooked on Classics, and realized you don't mess with an already great thing. It's really the perfect sandwich as it is. While the Mornay sauce is classic, the sandwich is a little lighter and still delicious without it.

Makes 1 sandwich

1 egg

1 tablespoon butter

2 slices rustic country bread

2 teaspoons Dijon mustard

2 slices ham

½ cup grated Gruyère cheese

Mornay Sauce (optional; recipe follows)

Salt and freshly ground pepper

» In a skillet large enough to hold the 2 slices of bread side by side, fry the egg sunny-side up. Set the egg aside on a plate and increase the heat to medium-low. Add the butter and let it melt. Place both slices of bread in the skillet and top one of them with the mustard and ham and the other with the cheese. Toast the bread for about 2 minutes, until it's golden brown. Carefully remove the ham-topped slice from the pan and place it on a plate. Spoon on some of the sauce and then top it with the other slice of bread (no flipping needed!), then the egg, and a bit more sauce if desired. Season to taste with salt and pepper.

MORNAY SAUCE

Makes about 1 cup

1 tablespoon unsalted butter

1 tablespoon all-purpose flour

1 cup milk

Large pinch of salt and pepper

Pinch of freshly grated nutmeg

½ cup grated Gruyère cheese

» Melt the butter in a small, heavy-bottomed saucepan over medium-high heat. Whisk in the flour and cook, stirring constantly, about 1 minute, being careful not to let it brown. Whisk in the milk, bring it to a low boil, and cook, stirring constantly, about 2 minutes more. Add the salt, pepper, and nutmeg. Remove the pan from the heat and stir in the cheese until it melts. Use immediately or cool, cover, and refrigerate for up to 3 days.

my ultimate burger

Dick's Kitchen in Portland features a rotating "guest burger" on its menu with meats that range from buffalo to duck+pork (aka dork) to wild boar. They're always good, but I find myself coming back to a beef burger, especially one that's made with great-quality, grass-fed beef. By grinding the meat yourself, you know exactly what you're getting.

Makes 1 burger

» Cut the sirloin into 1-inch chunks and the bacon into 1-inch pieces. Place in a meat grinder and grind twice. If you're using preground meat, you can just stir it together with finely chopped, uncooked bacon.

» In a small bowl, mix the ground meat with 1 of the eggs, shallots, bread crumbs, paprika, and salt and pepper to taste. Form the mixture into a ball, then gently press to flatten it into a 4-inch disc.

» Grill the burger on an outdoor grill for 5 to 7 minutes on each side (depending on your doneness preference). If you don't have an outdoor grill, try using a cast-iron stovetop grill pan greased with a small amount of oil. Add the cheese during the last few minutes of cooking.

» While the burger is cooking, toast the bun and fry the remaining egg over easy.

» Spread the ketchup, mustard, and/or mayo on the bottom of the bun. Follow with the pickles and lettuce. Place the burger on top of the lettuce, cheese side up, and top with the tomato, onion, and egg. Gently add the top of the bun.

¼ pound sirloin

2 strips bacon (optional)

2 eggs

1 small shallot, chopped

2 tablespoons bread crumbs

Pinch of smoked paprika

Salt and freshly ground pepper

1 slice cheddar cheese

1 brioche bun

Ketchup, mustard, and/or mayo (optional)

Pickles (optional)

1 leaf butterhead lettuce (optional)

1 slice tomato (optional)

1 slice red onion (optional)

sunny-side chili

You can do chili slow and you can do chili quick. This is the quick version, which was my husband's typical Thursday-night dinner growing up, served with a stack of toast on the side. Clearly, he isn't from Texas, but that doesn't make this chili any less delicious. You'll want to use a really good chile powder for this recipe since that is the major flavor; I love the New Mexican Red Chile Powder from Rancho Gordo.

Makes 2 bowls

» Heat the oil in a medium saucepan over medium-low heat and add the onion, celery, bell pepper, and garlic. Cook, stirring frequently, until they're lightly softened, about 5 minutes.

» Increase the heat to medium-high and crumble in the ground beef. Cook for about 5 minutes, or until the meat has browned. Add the salt and pepper to taste, Worcestershire, chile powder, and beans. Cook for about 2 minutes, then add the tomato juice. Bring to a boil, then reduce the heat to maintain a gentle simmer. Cook for about 10 minutes.

» While the chili is simmering, toast and butter the bread, and fry the eggs sunny-side up.

» To serve, divide the chili between two bowls and top each with an egg. Serve with the toast on the side; Cam and I always make a big stack with the buttered sides together.

1 teaspoon olive oil

½ cup diced onion

1 celery stalk, diced

2 slices green bell pepper, diced

1 clove garlic, minced

½ pound lean ground beef

Salt and freshly ground pepper

Dash of Worcestershire sauce

2 tablespoons chile powder

1 (7-ounce) can red kidney beans, drained

½ cup tomato juice

6 slices sandwich bread

2 eggs

grilled cheese and egg sandwich

This one is a little trickier than it sounds, because it requires you to cook the egg and bread in the same skillet—some flipping is involved—but an egg on your grilled cheese is an unexpectedly amazing upgrade.

Makes 1 sandwich

» Melt the butter over medium-low heat in a skillet big enough to hold the two slices of bread side by side. When it has just melted (not browned), place a slice of bread on one side of the skillet and gently pour the egg on the other side. Top the bread with the cheese. Cut a yolk-size hole in the middle of the other bread slice and carefully top the egg with that slice, lining up the yolk and the hole. Add a little more butter to the pan if it looks dry.

» Now, very carefully, use a spatula to flip the piece of bread with the egg under it. Place the cheese-covered slice on top. Let the sandwich cook for another minute to brown, then lift it out of the pan, flipping so that the egg side is up.

1 tablespoon butter

2 slices sourdough bread

2 slices American cheese

1 egg

kimchi fried rice

Inspired by one of my favorite food trucks in Seattle, Marination Mobile, this fried rice is spicy, with a bit of crunch from the cashews. When it's in *my* bowl, I top it with two over-easy eggs and a little more kimchi on the side.

Makes 2 hearty servings

2 tablespoons vegetable oil, divided

1 yellow onion, diced

4 green onions, white and light-green parts, chopped

1 large carrot, finely diced

8 ounces shiitake mushrooms, stemmed and sliced

2 cloves garlic, minced

½ cup kimchi, plus more for serving

1 tablespoon minced fresh ginger

3 cups cooked, cooled rice

1 tablespoon soy sauce

1 tablespoon sriracha (optional)

¼ cup cashews, chopped (optional)

2 to 4 eggs

» Heat 1 tablespoon of the oil in a large wok over medium-high heat. Add the onion, green onions, and carrot, and cook until lightly softened, about 2 minutes. Remove the veggies from the wok and lightly wipe it out with a paper towel.

» Return the wok to the heat and add the remaining tablespoon oil, along with the mushrooms and garlic. Stir-fry for about 2 minutes, or until the shiitakes soften and become a little glossy. Chop the kimchi. Add the onion mixture back to the wok, along with the ginger and kimchi.

» Add the rice and stir to distribute. Increase the heat slightly and let the rice sit so some of it crisps on the bottom of the wok. Pour in the soy sauce and sriracha and stir to combine. Stir in the cashews. Reduce the heat to medium-low. In a separate skillet, fry the eggs over easy.

» To serve, divide the rice between 2 bowls and top each bowl with 1 or 2 eggs and additional kimchi on the side.

duck egg sandwich with spinach and chipotle cream

Feed this luscious sandwich to your egg-eating veggie friends when they get a burger craving, and they'll likely think twice about ever ordering a veggie burger–puck again. When you eat it, it drips and spills everywhere in a decidedly appealing way. **NOTE:** The bun must be fresh. *Really* fresh. A stale bun will wreck this sandwich.

Makes 1 sandwich

1 tablespoon adobo sauce (from a can of chipotles; add more or less depending on how spicy you like things)

1 tablespoon sour cream

1 brioche bun, toasted

1 duck egg

½ cup baby spinach or arugula

1 to 2 strips smoked red pepper

1 to 2 rings red onion

» Mix the adobo sauce with the sour cream. Spread the mixture on both sides of the bun. Fry the egg sunny-side up. Top the bottom of the bun with the spinach, red pepper, onion, and egg. Add the top bun and serve immediately.

lunch breakfast burrito bowl

After several years of carb overload from testing recipes for my books *Doughnuts* and *Real Snacks*, it was time for a carb reset. During several weeks of low-carb eating, this was my go-to food (sans the potatoes). Full of flavor and protein, and customizable to the nth degree, it's so good, I didn't miss the carbs at all.

Makes 1 bowl

1 medium Yukon Gold potato

Olive oil for cooking potatoes

Salt and freshly ground pepper

2 eggs

½ cup cooked black beans

1 serrano pepper, seeded and finely chopped

2 tablespoons chopped fresh cilantro, divided

Pico de gallo

2 tablespoons crumbled *cotija* cheese

» Cut the potato into ½-inch chunks and put them in a pot of cold water. Bring the water to a boil over medium-high heat and cook for 5 minutes, until just a little tender. Drain the potatoes and transfer them to a skillet with a splash of olive oil. Season them to taste with salt and pepper, and cook over medium-high heat until the edges are gorgeously crisp.

» In a small bowl, whisk or blend the eggs with an immersion blender and pour them over the potatoes. Stir, gently and infrequently, until you have nice, fluffy, eggy bits mixed with your crispy potatoes. Turn off the heat as soon as the eggs have set.

» Warm the beans, pepper, and 1 tablespoon of the cilantro in a small saucepan over medium-low heat. Transfer the bean mixture to a bowl, top with the potatoes and eggs, and add the remaining tablespoon cilantro, pico de gallo to taste, and cheese.

blt&e

Made with an over-hard egg, this is the perfect sandwich to eat on the go without fear of getting egg on your face.

Makes 1 sandwich

» Toast the bread and fry the bacon and the egg, over hard. Place 1 slice of the lettuce on the toast and top with the tomato. Next comes the egg. Cut the bacon in half and place on the egg. Season to taste with salt and pepper. Add the other piece of lettuce, followed by the other piece of toast. Slice in half and serve.

2 slices sourdough bread

1 strip bacon

1 egg

2 leaves butterhead lettuce

1 slice tomato

Salt and freshly ground pepper

MAINS

---

winner, winner, eggs
for dinner!

white beans with bacon, poached eggs, and harissa butter

It's a safe bet that Sitka & Spruce, one of my favorite Seattle restaurants, will have some dish on the menu with an egg on it. It's a sure thing I'll order it. I based this recipe on one of my S&S favorites. With canned beans, it's simple enough to pull together for a quick yet elegant dinner; if you have a bit more time, make it from dried beans that you simmer slowly with a bit of thyme and garlic for hours, until the beans are perfectly creamy.

Makes 2 light dinner servings

» Poach the eggs and set them aside to drain while you prepare the rest of the dish.

» Heat a medium skillet over medium-high heat. Chop the bacon into ¼-inch-wide pieces, add them to the skillet, and cook until crispy. Transfer the bacon to a paper towel–lined plate, leaving the drippings in the skillet. Add the broccoli rabe with the salt, and sauté until the color brightens and the rabe softens a little, about 3 minutes. Set it aside in a bowl. Add the beans, tomatoes, and bacon, reduce the heat to medium, and cook (don't overstir or you'll crush the beans) for about 2 minutes, until hot.

» In a separate skillet, brown the butter and stir in the harissa.

» Divide the bean mixture between 2 bowls and top with the broccoli rabe, followed by the eggs. Pour the harissa butter over the eggs. Sprinkle with a bit of flaked sea salt and serve immediately.

2 eggs

1 strip thick-cut bacon

1 cup chopped broccoli rabe

Pinch of salt

1 (14-ounce) can cannellini beans or other white beans, drained

8 to 10 cherry tomatoes

2 tablespoons unsalted butter

1 teaspoon harissa

Maldon or other flaked sea salt

thin-crust white pie

A hot pizza stone will give this crust a lovely crispness, but if you don't have one, a heated baking sheet will do. If you don't have time to make your own crust, this recipe works great with high-quality, uncooked store-bought crust as well—just start it at the point where you roll out the dough. **NOTE:** If you're making your own crust, you'll need to allow time for the dough to rest in the refrigerator overnight. (Dough can be made up to three days ahead.)

Makes 3 medium pizzas

¾ cup warm (115 degrees F) water

½ teaspoon active dry yeast

5 tablespoons olive oil, divided

2¼ cups bread or all-purpose flour, divided, plus more for dusting

½ teaspoon salt

Semolina or cornmeal for dusting

½ cup Parmesan cheese, divided

3 teaspoons dried oregano, divided

Red pepper flakes

Maldon or other flaked sea salt

9 eggs

» Place the water in the bowl of a stand mixer fitted with a dough hook. Sprinkle the yeast on top and let it sit for 5 minutes. Add 2 tablespoons of the oil, sprinkle about ½ cup of the flour over the top, and mix with a fork. Add another ½ cup of flour, stir, and repeat until the dough just starts to pull together in a sticky blob.

» When the dough has come together, add the salt and mix on low speed, adding about ¼ cup flour at a time, until the dough pulls away cleanly from the sides of the bowl, about 5 to 7 minutes. You'll have a bit of flour left over.

» Dust a clean work surface with a small handful of flour. Place the dough (it will be a touch sticky) in the middle, sprinkle it with a bit more flour, and knead it for 4 or 5 strokes, forming a smooth ball. Cut the dough into 3 equal pieces, roll them into balls, and dust each with more flour. Place each ball in a plastic bag (be sure to allow room for the dough to expand) and refrigerate overnight (and up to 3 days). If you don't want to make all your pizzas at once, the dough can be frozen, then thawed when needed.

» When you're ready to make the pizzas, remove the dough from the refrigerator. Generously flour a clean work surface and place the dough balls on it. Turn them over once and gently press each into a 5-inch circle. Cover with plastic wrap and let them rest at room temperature for 1 hour.

» Preheat the oven to 500 degrees F and place a pizza stone or baking sheet on the middle rack.

» Working with one dough ball at a time, dimple it all over with your fingertips, then roll it from the middle out into a 10- to 12-inch circle, dusting the board and rolling pin with flour as needed. Create a small moat about ½ inch from the edge around the entire crust (this will help contain the eggs). Brush about 1 tablespoon of oil over the top.

» Sprinkle a pizza peel or the bottom-side of a baking sheet dusted with liberally with semolina. Lift the crust onto the peel, then give the peel a shake to make sure the crust will slide off easily before you add your toppings. Sprinkle one-third of the Parmesan, 1 teaspoon oregano, and red pepper flakes and sea salt to taste over the crust, distributing evenly. Arrange 3 eggs around the crust, spacing them evenly.

» Quickly transfer the pizza to the hot pizza stone or baking sheet. Bake until the crust is golden on the edges and the eggs have set, 5 to 8 minutes, rotating once if needed. Remove the pizza from the oven and let it sit for 2 minutes before slicing. Drizzle with a nice fruity olive oil before serving.

egg-topped deep-dish pizza

This recipe uses an airy focaccia-like dough paired with a rich Italian tomato sauce and much less cheese than you'd find on a heavy Chicago-style pie. The egg adds a lovely creaminess without all the heavy, oily cheese. You bake this pie right in a cast-iron skillet, so there's no need for special equipment such as a pizza stone or deep-dish pan.

Makes 1 medium pizza or 3 small ones

» Put the water and yeast in a bowl and whisk slightly to combine. Stir in ½ cup of the flour and mix for 1 minute to create a wet batter. This is called a sponge. Cover and let sit at room temperature for 1 hour.

» Transfer the sponge to the bowl of a stand mixer fitted with the hook attachment and add the sugar and olive oil. Use a wooden spoon to loosely incorporate. Add the remaining cup of flour and the salt to the bowl. Mix the dough on low speed for 3 minutes or knead by hand for about 15 minutes. Lightly flour a clean work surface and place the dough on it. Knead for another minute, turning the dough 90 degrees after each stroke, and form the dough into a smooth ball.

» Lightly grease a large cast-iron skillet (or 3 small skillets). Place the dough in the skillet, cover with a towel, and let it rest for 30 minutes.

» Preheat the oven to 425 degrees F.

» When the dough has rested, lightly grease your fingers and, working from the middle, press the dough up the sides of the skillet. Cover it again and let it rest for another 30 minutes, then uncover, dimple it with lightly oiled fingers all along the bottom of the skillet, place the skillet in the oven, and bake for 10 minutes.

½ cup warm (115 degrees F) water

½ teaspoon active dry yeast

1½ cups bread flour

1 tablespoon sugar

⅓ cup olive oil

½ teaspoon salt

⅓ cup grated mozzarella cheese

⅔ cup Tomato Sauce, cooled (recipe follows)

3 eggs

¼ cup grated Parmesan cheese

Maldon or other flaked sea salt

continued

» Remove the crust from the oven and cover the bottom with the mozzarella, tomato sauce, and any other toppings you desire. Bake for 10 to 15 minutes more, until the crust just turns golden.

» Carefully remove the pizza from the oven and arrange the eggs on top, spacing them evenly. Sprinkle with the Parmesan cheese and sea salt to taste. Return the pizza to the oven, and cook for another 10 to 12 minutes, until the eggs have set. Let the pizza cool for 5 minutes before slicing.

TOMATO SAUCE

¼ cup olive oil

¼ cup finely chopped onion

2 cloves garlic, smashed and finely chopped

Pinch of red pepper flakes

1 teaspoon dried basil

1 teaspoon dried oregano

1 (24-ounce) jar pureed San Marzano tomatoes

½ teaspoon salt

This recipe makes more than you'll need for the pizza. Freeze the extra sauce to make more pizzas, or use it in Spinach and Egg Lasagna (page 115).

Makes about 3 cups

» To make the sauce, heat the oil in a medium heavy-bottomed skillet over medium-low heat. Add the onions and cook for 3 minutes to soften. Add the garlic and cook for another 3 to 4 minutes. Add the red pepper flakes, basil, oregano, tomato puree, salt, and 1 cup water. Bring to a gentle boil over medium-high heat, then reduce the heat to low and simmer the sauce for about 45 minutes, or until it has reduced to 2 cups. (For a less chunky sauce, puree with an immersion blender or in a blender.)

spinach and egg lasagna

You can make this lasagna in a traditional large casserole dish, but I like the extra-crunchy edges you get by making individual lasagnas, and there's no worry about slicing through an egg yolk while serving.

Makes 6 individual lasagnas

» Preheat the oven to 375 degrees F. Lightly butter the sides of 6 individual casserole or other baking dishes big enough to hold a lasagna noodle and place them on a baking sheet. Fill a large pan or bowl with ice water and set aside.

» Bring about 4 quarts of water to a boil in a large pot (or work in batches). Add the oil and boil the noodles until they are al dente, 8 to 10 minutes. Drain the noodles and transfer them to the ice water–filled pan to quickly cool. When the noodles are cool, dry them between 2 kitchen towels.

» Spread 1 tablespoon of the béchamel on the bottom of each of the prepared casserole dishes. Layer each dish with a lasagna noodle, then 2 tablespoons ricotta cheese and a handful of baby spinach leaves, followed by another noodle, 2 tablespoons tomato sauce, a handful of mozzarella, and 2 tablespoons béchamel. Repeat this sequence once, then add another noodle, another 2 tablespoons sauce, and some more mozzarella, ending with a sprinkling of Parmesan.

» Cover the dishes with aluminum foil and bake for 20 minutes. Uncover, place an egg on top of each, drizzle on some more béchamel, and sprinkle with a bit more Parmesan. Return dishes to the oven and bake for another 10 to 15 minutes, or until the eggs have set.

Butter for greasing dishes

1 tablespoon olive oil

30 (4-by-6-inch) lasagna noodles

Béchamel Sauce (recipe follows)

1½ cups fresh ricotta cheese

1 (5-ounce) package baby spinach leaves

1½ cups Tomato Sauce (page 114)

3 cups shredded mozzarella cheese

¾ cup finely grated Parmesan cheese

6 eggs

BÉCHAMEL SAUCE

Makes about 2 cups sauce

» In a medium saucepan, melt the butter over medium-low heat. Sprinkle the flour over the butter and whisk until smooth. Continue cooking over medium heat until the flour just starts to color, about 5 minutes. Whisk in the milk ¼ cup at a time and bring to a low boil. Whisk constantly until the sauce thickens, about 10 minutes. Add the salt, pepper, and nutmeg to taste.

2 tablespoons unsalted butter

2 tablespoons all-purpose flour

2 cups milk, warmed to 110 degrees F

Salt and freshly ground pepper

Freshly grated nutmeg

spaghetti with wilted greens and walnut pesto

Walnuts add a lovely mellowness to this herby pesto, which melts beautifully when stirred into warm pasta. For an extra-green version, try substituting pistachios for the walnuts.

Makes 4 servings

» Cook the spaghetti according to the package directions to al dente in a large pot of lightly salted water. Drain the pasta, reserving 1 cup of the pasta water.

» Add the walnuts, parsley, basil, garlic, and Parmesan to a food processor, and pulse to finely chop. Stream in 2 tablespoons of the oil to create a chunky puree. Add salt to taste.

» Preheat the oven to 350 degrees F. While the oven heats, fry the eggs sunny-side up and set aside. Place the tomatoes on a baking sheet and roast for 5 to 10 minutes, until they begin to burst.

» In a large skillet over medium-high heat, add the remaining tablespoon of olive oil, toss in the kale, and cook until it's just wilted, about 2 minutes. Reduce the heat to medium, add the drained pasta, and cook for 2 minutes, or until warmed through. Stir in the pesto with about ½ cup of the pasta water and cook until the water has evaporated.

» Divide the pasta among 4 bowls and top each with an egg, add one-forth of the cherry tomatoes, and a sprinkle of Parmesan and red pepper flakes to taste.

1 pound spinach spaghetti

½ cup chopped and toasted walnuts

½ cup chopped Italian parsley

¼ cup chopped fresh basil leaves

1 clove garlic, chopped

¼ cup shredded Parmesan, plus more for garnish

3 tablespoons olive oil, divided

Salt

4 eggs

1 pint cherry tomatoes (optional)

1 package (5 ounces) baby kale or other braising greens

Red pepper flakes (optional)

chicken and egg potpie

When I originally envisioned this recipe, I pictured a flaky crust with a runny egg yolk just poking through a hole in the center, concealing an egg within. Then I tried to figure out how exactly to make that happen, so the crust would be perfectly golden and the egg not a hard mess. I soon discovered that it was even more beautiful with the white of the egg draped over the entire top, held in by the crimped crust edges. What's even better is that this technique can be easily applied to store-bought potpies, if you don't feel like making your own.

Makes 4 individual potpies

2½ cups all-purpose flour

1 cup (2 sticks) unsalted butter, chopped into 1-inch cubes, cold

½ teaspoon salt

2 to 3 tablespoons ice water

1 teaspoon olive oil

2 boneless, skinless chicken thighs, chopped into ½- inch cubes

¼ cup chopped onion

1 cup quartered mushrooms

1 stalk celery, diced

1 carrot, diced

2 cups chicken stock

2 tablespoons chopped Italian parsley

1 tablespoon cornstarch

½ cup peas

Freshly ground pepper

4 eggs

» Sift the flour into the bowl of a food processor. Add the butter and salt, and pulse until crumbly. Add the water, a tablespoon at a time, pulsing to combine until the dough comes together in a ball. (Or make the dough by hand, cutting in the butter with two forks or your fingers.) Wrap the dough in plastic wrap and refrigerate for at least 30 minutes.

» In a heavy medium pot, heat the oil over medium-high heat. Add the chicken, working in batches to keep from overcrowding the pan, and sear on all sides until golden, about 3 minutes total. Add the onions, mushrooms, celery, and carrot and cook for 2 minutes. Add ½ cup of the stock and scrape off any browned bits on the bottom of the pan. Add the remaining stock and parsley, and bring to a boil. Reduce the heat and gently simmer for 15 minutes, until the carrots have softened. Mix the cornstarch with ¼ cup water, and stir it into the pot. Continue to cook until the mixture thickens. Add the peas, and season to taste with salt and pepper. Remove from heat and set aside to cool.

» Preheat the oven to 400 degrees F.

» Divide the crust into 8 pieces, and form each into a ball. On a lightly floured work surface, roll out the balls into 6-inch rounds. Place 1 round in the bottom of a 5-inch pie tin so the pastry edges overhang the sides. Repeat with 3 more of the rounds. Cut a 1-inch-diameter hole from the middle of the remaining 4 rounds.

» Spoon about 1 cup of the cooled filling into each pie tin. Cover each with 1 of the cut-out rounds, centering the hole. Pinch the edges of the top and bottom crusts together so they stand about ¾ of an inch above the top of the pastry, forming a little wall.

» Bake the potpies until the crusts are golden and the filling bubbly, about 25 minutes. Using a small spoon, carefully reach in through the hole in the crust and push the filling aside a little to create a small well. Pour an egg into each hole; the yolk should sit in the hole, but the white will run over the top of the crust. Bake the potpies for another 10 to 15 minutes, until the eggs set. Cool for about 5 minutes before serving.

tomato risotto with poached duck eggs

If you've ever found yourself torn between pasta *pomodoro* and risotto in an Italian restaurant, as I have many times, this dish is the perfect solution. It has all the creaminess of risotto with the luscious flavor of a buttery tomato sauce. A poached duck egg on top pushes the whole thing onto my list of heavenly dinners.

Makes 4 servings

» Melt the butter in a large, heavy-bottomed skillet over medium-low heat. Add the shallot and cook slowly until soft and translucent, about 5 minutes. Add the rice, stirring with a wooden spoon to coat each grain. Cook for about 5 minutes, until the rice becomes mostly translucent. Add the wine and cook until the liquid has been absorbed, about 3 minutes. Add the tomato puree and cook for about 5 minutes. Start adding the stock, ½ cup at a time, letting the liquid completely absorb before adding the next ½ cup, until the rice is creamy but not mushy. Season to taste with salt and pepper.

» Poach the duck eggs and set them aside. While they are cooking, in a small skillet, fry the pancetta until crispy and drain on a paper towel–lined plate to wick off any excess oil.

» Divide the risotto among 4 bowls and sprinkle with Parmesan. Top with a duck egg and the pancetta and garnish with the basil.

2 tablespoons unsalted butter

1 shallot, finely chopped

1 cup arborio rice

½ cup white wine

½ cup San Marzano tomato puree

4 cups chicken or vegetable stock, warmed to 120 degrees F

Salt and freshly ground pepper

4 duck eggs

4 pieces pancetta

Freshly grated Parmesan, for garnish

¼ cup fresh small basil leaves, for garnish

abura soba

There's nothing quite like sitting elbow to elbow in a little steamy basement restaurant in Japan for an enormous bowl of brothy ramen. But a huge bowl of abura soba—a no-broth ramen packed with flavor from kimchi, pork belly, and a runny-yolked egg—at Wafu in Portland certainly comes close. Dried noodles (ditching the flavor packet) are fine in a pinch, but for the perfect ramen noodle bite, look for *nama* ("raw") ramen in the fresh or frozen section of Asian markets.

You can cook the pork belly up to three days ahead of time, cool it, and keep it tightly wrapped in the refrigerator until you need it. Then just reheat it in a 350-degree oven for about 15 minutes.

Makes 2 large bowls

1 (2-by-1-inch) piece (4 ounces) pork belly

1 teaspoon salt

½ carrot

½ cup rice wine vinegar

1 tablespoon mirin

2 eggs

8 ounces fresh ramen noodles

2 teaspoons sesame oil

1-inch-long piece daikon, grated

1 green onion, sliced

½ cup kimchi

1 tablespoon sambal oelek or sri racha hot sauce

Togarashi or other red pepper flakes (optional)

» Preheat the oven to 350 degrees F.

» Heat a large skillet over medium heat. Score the fat side of the pork belly, rub with salt and place it (fat side down) in the hot skillet. Fry it for 2 minutes to render some of the fat. Transfer the belly, fat side up, to a large, ovenproof skillet and roast for 1 hour, or until it measures 145 degrees F on a meat thermometer in the center. Let it rest for 5 minutes.

» While the belly roasts, julienne the carrot and place the sticks in a bowl with the vinegar and mirin.

» Slice the pork belly into ¼-inch-thick slices. Drain the carrots from the vinegar. Fry the eggs sunnyside or over easy and set aside.

» Bring 2 quarts of water to a boil in a large soup pot, and cook the noodles for 5 minutes, or until al dente. Drain the noodles and divide between 2 bowls. Sprinkle with the sesame oil and distribute the pork belly slices, pickled carrot, daikon, green onion, kimchi and sambal oelek around the noodles. Slide an egg on top of each. Sprinkle with a bit of togarashi to taste and serve.

new mexico–style "christmas" enchiladas

My father's enchiladas was the dish that started me down the path of putting eggs on top. A good-quality canned enchilada sauce is a fine choice (it's what we usually used), but you can elevate your enchiladas by making your own sauces and serving them "Christmas-style": smothered in half red chile sauce and half green.

Makes 4 enchiladas

Red Chile Sauce (recipe follows)

Green Chile Sauce (recipe follows)

¼ cup vegetable oil, plus more as needed for frying

12 corn tortillas

1 cup shredded cheddar cheese

½ cup finely chopped onion

4 eggs

½ cup sour cream (optional)

» Preheat the oven to 250 degrees F and have 4 oven-proof plates nearby. Warm both chile sauces and set them by the plates.

» Heat the oil in a large skillet over medium heat. Working with one at a time, add a tortilla to the hot oil and fry on both sides, about 1 minute each side. Immediately dip the tortilla in the red chile sauce, and place it on a plate. Top with a bit of cheese (not too much!) and onion. Fry another tortilla, dip it in the red chile sauce, and place it on top, with a bit more cheese and onion, followed by one final fried and dipped tortilla. Move the plate to the oven to keep it warm while you prepare the other plates.

» When you've made all the enchiladas, fry the eggs sunny-side up. Top each enchilada with an egg, then cover half with more red chile sauce and the other half with green chile sauce. Divide the sour cream among the enchiladas and serve.

RED CHILE SAUCE

Makes about 2 cups

10 dried guajillo chiles, stemmed and seeded

1 tablespoon olive oil

3 whole cloves garlic, peeled

Salt

» Place the chiles in a small bowl, and add boiling water to cover. Let soak for 10 minutes to soften.

» Heat a small skillet with the olive oil over medium-low heat and sauté the garlic until it's golden and softened, about 2 minutes.

» Remove the chiles from the water and place them in a food processor or blender with a few tablespoons of the chile water, the oil and the garlic. Puree until smooth, adding a bit more chile water as needed. Transfer to a medium saucepan and simmer the sauce for 20 minutes. Add salt to taste.

GREEN CHILE SAUCE

Makes about 2 cups

1 tablespoon olive oil

2 cloves garlic, minced

2 (4-ounce) cans diced green chiles

½ cup seeded and diced plum tomatoes

1 tablespoon all-purpose flour

Salt

» Heat a small skillet with the olive oil over medium-low heat and sauté the garlic until it's golden and softened, about 2 minutes. Add the chiles, tomatoes, and flour. Stir to combine, then add 1 cup of water. Simmer until the sauce reduces to a stew-like consistency, about 15 minutes. Season with salt to taste.

pan-fried catfish with creamed mushrooms and poached eggs

I like catfish for this simple pan-fried dish, but the punch of vinegar in the creamy mushroom sauce brings any thinly filleted white fish, such as sole, trout, or tilapia, to life.

Makes 2 servings

» Preheat the oven to 250 degrees F.

» In a shallow bowl or on a plate, mix the flour, salt, and pepper. Lightly dredge both sides of each fillet in the flour mixture.

» Heat 1 tablespoon of the oil in a medium cast-iron skillet over medium-high heat. When the oil is shimmering, add the catfish fillets. Fry for about 1 minute, then flip and fry for another minute on the other side, until just a little bit golden. Carefully transfer the fillets to an ovenproof plate and place in the oven to keep warm.

» Poach the eggs and set them aside to drain.

» While the eggs are poaching, add the remaining tablespoon of oil to the pan and increase the heat to high. Add the mushrooms and cook until they're softened and slightly caramelized, about 3 minutes. Reduce the heat to low and add the vinegar, using a spoon to scrape off any bits from the bottom of the pan. Add the crème fraîche and continue to cook until the sauce has reduced and become glossy.

» To serve, place a poached egg on each fillet, then top with half of the mushrooms and sauce. Careful, plates will be hot.

2 tablespoons corn flour (or all-purpose flour)

¼ teaspoon salt

¼ teaspoon freshly ground pepper

2 catfish fillets

2 tablespoons grapeseed or olive oil, divided

2 eggs

2 cups sliced assorted mushrooms

2 tablespoons sherry vinegar

¼ cup crème fraîche

buttermilk fried chicken and eggs

Soaking the chicken in buttermilk adds a bit of tang and tenderizes the meat, so if you can, let it soak overnight. If you're pressed for time, you can skip this step and simply dip the chicken in a shallow bowl of buttermilk before dipping in the flour.

Makes 4 servings

» Rinse the chicken, then place it in a resealable plastic bag. Pour 2 cups of the buttermilk over the top and seal, pressing all the air out. Refrigerate for a few hours or overnight.

» When you're done marinating the chicken, poach the eggs and set them aside to drain and cool.

» In a shallow bowl, mix the flour, panko, garlic powder, paprika, cayenne, salt, and pepper.

» Heat at least 2 inches of oil in a large skillet to 350 degrees F. Remove the chicken from the buttermilk and dredge the thighs in the flour mixture. Fry each piece (in batches if necessary; don't overcrowd the pan) for about 7 minutes each side, until golden brown all over. The interior temperature of the meat should be 165 degrees F. Set the chicken aside on a paper towel–lined plate to drain.

4 boneless chicken thighs

2 cups buttermilk, plus a little more for brushing

4 eggs

1 cup all-purpose flour

½ cup panko (Japanese bread crumbs)

1 teaspoon garlic powder

½ teaspoon hot paprika

½ teaspoon cayenne

1 teaspoon salt

½ teaspoon freshly ground pepper

Safflower oil for frying

» Carefully brush each egg with a bit of buttermilk and dredge the cooled poached eggs in the flour mixture. Fry for about 1 minute on each side until golden brown and crisp.

» Serve each piece of chicken with the fried/poached egg on top. Even better? Put the chicken on your favorite buttermilk biscuit for the ultimate down-home brunch.

brined pork chops with fried eggs and jalapeño butter

High-quality pork chops, such as those from Carlton Farms, when lightly brined make a great weeknight alternative to more indulgent (and expensive) steak and eggs. Just make sure you use thick-cut (aka double-cut) chops, which are much harder to dry out than the more classic thin-cut chops.

Makes 2 servings

4 cups water

¼ cup kosher salt

¼ cup brown sugar

1 bay leaf

2 teaspoons apple cider vinegar

2 (8-ounce) thick-cut pork chops

2 tablespoons (1 medium) chopped jalapeño

4 tablespoons (½ stick) unsalted butter, at room temperature

¼ teaspoon sea salt

Olive oil for brushing chops

Salt and freshly ground pepper

2 eggs

» Make a brine by mixing the water with the salt, sugar, bay leaf, and vinegar. Stir until the sugar and salt mostly dissolve.

» Place the pork chops in a gallon-size resealable plastic bag and carefully pour the brine over the top. Seal and let refrigerate for 1 to 2 hours (and no more than 12 hours).

» In a food processor, or with a mortar and pestle, blend the jalapeño, butter, and sea salt.

» Remove the chops from the brine and pat dry with a paper towel. Brush the chops with olive oil and season to taste with salt and pepper on both sides.

» Heat a grill pan on medium (or use an outdoor grill). Grill the chops until the internal temperature reaches about 150 degrees F on a meat thermometer. Remove them from the heat and top each with 2 tablespoons of the jalapeño butter. Allow the chops to rest for at least 5 minutes while you fry the eggs.

» Fry the eggs sunny-side up and serve one on top of each chop.

SWEETS

---

i just keep egging
you on

maple meringue doughnut holes

What's better than a sweet and fluffy doughnut? One stuffed with sweet and fluffy maple meringue! I make these as large doughnut holes, since they're quite rich, but feel free to cut them with a 2½-inch cutter to make regular-size doughnuts.

Makes about 20 small doughnuts

» In a medium bowl, dissolve 1 teaspoon of the yeast into ¼ cup of the milk. Add ¼ cup of the bread flour and stir to create a smooth paste. Cover with plastic wrap and let rest in a warm spot for 30 minutes.

» Combine the remaining ¼ cup milk and 1 teaspoon yeast in another medium bowl. (If you have a stand mixer, you can use it, but I made this batch with a wooden spoon and a bit of good old-fashioned stirring.) Add the rested flour paste along with the vanilla and the egg. Stir until smooth. Add the whole wheat flour plus another ¼ cup of the bread flour. Add the sugar and salt, and vigorously stir until the dough starts to come together. Add the butter and continue to stir, adding more bread flour about ⅛ cup at a time, until the dough starts to form into a ball. Then, with a dough hook if you're using a stand mixer, or with your hands, knead in the remaining bread flour a little at a time until the dough is somewhat smooth and only a little sticky. You may have a little flour left over; save it for when you roll out the dough.

» Cover the bowl with plastic wrap and let it sit in a warm place for 30 minutes. After it has rested, gently punch down the dough, cover it again, and refrigerate it for at least 1 hour (and up to 12 hours). This will help stiffen the dough a little and make it easier to roll and cut out.

2 teaspoons active dry yeast, divided

½ cup whole milk, heated to 110 degrees F, divided

1 to 1¼ cups bread flour, divided

½ teaspoon vanilla extract

1 egg

¼ cup whole wheat flour

1 tablespoon cane sugar

¼ teaspoon salt

2 tablespoons unsalted butter, softened

4 cups safflower oil

Maple Meringue Filling (recipe follows)

continued

» Line a baking sheet with a lightly floured dish towel (not terry cloth). With a lightly floured rolling pin, roll out the dough on a lightly floured surface to ½ inch thick. Using a metal cookie cutter or small drinking glass dipped in flour, cut out 2-inch-diameter rounds.

» Place the doughnuts on the cloth-lined baking sheet at least 1 inch apart and cover with plastic wrap. Place the baking sheet in a warm spot and let it sit until the doughnuts almost double in size, about 30 to 40 minutes, testing at 5-minute intervals. (To determine whether the dough is ready, touch it lightly with a fingertip. If it springs back immediately, it needs more time. If it springs back slowly, it's ready. If it doesn't spring back at all, it has sat too long; you can punch it down and reroll it once.)

» When the doughnuts are almost done rising, heat a heavy-bottomed pot with at least 2 inches of the oil until a deep-fat thermometer registers 365 degrees F. With a metal spatula, carefully lift the doughnuts and place them in the oil. Fry for 1 to 2 minutes per side, or until light golden brown. Remove them with a slotted spoon and drain on a wire rack over a paper towel.

» It's important to let the doughnuts cool all the way before filling, but if you want them sugar coated, dip them in a shallow bowl of superfine sugar while they're still slightly warm to the touch. If you want to coat them in confectioners' sugar, wait for them to cool before dusting.

» These doughnuts become almost completely hollow when fried so they're really easy to fill. Just lightly hold the bottom of the doughnut, cradling the sides with your fingers, and gently insert the piping bag tip. (If the doughnut isn't hollow for some reason, you can clear space with a chopstick.) Simply squeeze the piping bag, slowly withdrawing it as you fill. I like a little dollop of filling to ooze from the top so you can see what's inside. If you'd like, use a kitchen torch to lightly brown the filling.

MAPLE MERINGUE FILLING

Makes about 2 cups meringue

1 cup maple syrup (Grade A or B)

2 egg whites

¼ teaspoon cream of tartar

Pinch of salt

» Put the maple syrup in a small, heavy-bottomed pot over medium heat with a candy thermometer attached. Heat until the syrup comes to 235 degrees F. It will bubble pretty fiercely, so keep an eye on it so it doesn't bubble over. Also, be careful not to overheat it or you'll end up with maple candy.

» When the syrup gets up to around 220 degrees F, place the egg whites, cream of tartar, and salt in the bowl of a stand mixer fitted with the paddle attachment and mix on medium speed until just frothy. (You can also use a hand mixer or whisk.) Increase the speed to high and beat until the whites hold a stiff peak.

» When the syrup has come to temperature, lower the mixer back to medium speed and slowly stream in the hot syrup, continuing to beat until the meringue is thick and a bit shiny, about 2 minutes.

» Transfer the meringue to a piping bag. A long éclair tip is the easiest, but a standard ¼-inch star tip will work well too. Fill the doughnuts as directed in the recipe.

orange and meringue "eggs"

These adorable sweets may look like your morning breakfast, but they taste absolutely like dessert. Take the time to get your baked meringues very dry for the easiest treats to eat—a little moisture trapped inside, and you'll end up with chewy (but still delicious) bites.

Makes about a dozen meringues

» Preheat the oven on its lowest temperature, around 170 degrees F is ideal.

» Spoon the meringue onto parchment-lined baking sheets in 3-inch rounds that resemble thick fried-egg whites. Make a shallow indentation in the center of each with the back of the spoon. Bake for 4 hours, propping the door open slightly, until the meringues are completely dry. Turn off the oven and let the meringues cool completely.

» Fill a large pan or bowl with ice water and set aside. Put the egg yolks, sugar, and salt in the top of a double boiler or in a small metal bowl and place over a pot of simmering water. Whisk until the mixture is well combined and warm. Add the orange zest and juice and stir with a spoon until the curd thickens to just about the consistency of a runny egg yolk. Remove the bowl from the heat and whisk in the vanilla and butter until completely combined and shiny. Place the bowl in the ice water–filled pan to quickly cool. (If any of the yolk has curdled, press the mixture through a fine-mesh sieve.) Refrigerate for at least 1 hour, until the curd has completely cooled.

» Fill the indentation in each meringue with a dollop of the orange curd and serve immediately. The meringues will keep, unfilled, for several days in a cookie tin (they may get chewy if stored in plastic wrap).

1 recipe Basic Meringue (page 18)

3 egg yolks

½ cup superfine sugar

¼ teaspoon salt

2 teaspoons finely grated orange zest

½ cup freshly squeezed orange juice (from 2 medium oranges)

1 teaspoon vanilla extract (optional)

2 tablespoons unsalted butter, cut into chunks

frozen strawberry soufflé

It's best to use fresh, peak-season strawberries for this fluffy, chilled soufflé. If you do use frozen strawberries, let them thaw slightly, coarsely puree all of them, and drain any excess juice.

Makes 6 servings

½ pound strawberries, hulled

½ cup plus 2 tablespoons sugar, divided

2 egg whites

1 teaspoon orange zest

2 teaspoons vanilla extract

1¾ cups heavy cream

⅔ recipe Basic Meringue (page 18)

» Coarsely chop 1 cup of the strawberries and sprinkle with 2 tablespoons of the sugar. Puree the remaining strawberries and set aside.

» Beat the egg whites using a stand mixer fitted with the whisk attachment until you have soft peaks. Stream in the remaining ½ cup of sugar and continue to beat, creating a stiff meringue, about 3 minutes. Transform the meringue to a large bowl. Using a rubber spatula, gently fold in the orange zest, vanilla, and strawberry puree. Drain the chopped strawberries and fold them in as well.

» Whip the cream until fluffy and fold it into the meringue mixture.

» Spoon the soufflé mixture into ramekins, filling to just above the rim. Lightly cover and freeze overnight (or up to a week).

» Make the meringue topping just before you're ready to serve the soufflé.

» Using a pastry bag fitted with a ½-inch tip (or a resealable plastic bag with a corner cut off), pipe the meringue onto the frozen soufflés, and brown it lightly with a kitchen torch. Serve immediately.

lemon meringue "ice cream"

The beauty of a frozen meringue is that it stays creamy and easy to scoop even after days of freezing. This fluffy, frozen lemon meringue packs a lot of flavor, so a little scoop goes a long way.

Makes 8 to 10 servings

» To make the ice cream, fill a large pan or bowl with ice water and set aside. Put the egg yolks, sugar, and salt in the top of a double boiler or in a small metal bowl and place over a pot of simmering water. Whisk until the mixture is well combined and warm. Add the lemon zest and juice and stir with a spoon until the curd thickens to just about the consistency of a runny egg yolk. Remove the bowl from the heat and whisk in the vanilla and butter until the curd is thick and creamy. Place the bowl in the ice water–filled pan to quickly cool. (If any of the yolk has curdled, press the mixture through a fine-mesh sieve).

» Make the Basic Meringue and gently fold it into the lemon curd. Transfer the curd to a freezable container and chill until it firms slightly, about 1 hour.

» Make the meringue topping just before you're ready to serve the ice cream. Top each scoop with a dollop of meringue, browning it lightly with a kitchen torch. Serve immediately.

3 egg yolks, lightly beaten

½ cup superfine sugar

¼ teaspoon salt

2 teaspoons finely grated lemon zest

½ cup freshly squeezed lemon juice (from 3 medium lemons)

1 teaspoon vanilla extract (optional)

2 tablespoons unsalted butter, cut into chunks

1 recipe Basic Meringue (page 18), plus ⅔ recipe for garnish

chocolate malt meringue pie

If you only indulge in dessert now and then, you may as well go all out and make it this pie. The chocolate, the malt, the meringue . . . all favorites on their own, they become a magical cloud of deliciousness when mixed together. The only things missing are the puppies, rainbows, and unicorns.

Makes one 9-inch pie

» Whisk the sugar, cornstarch, salt, and egg yolks in a medium, heavy-bottomed saucepan until combined.

» In a small bowl, whisk the milk and ½ cup of the malt powder, then stream it into the egg mixture. Bring to a simmer over low heat, whisking constantly, until the mixture just thickens.

» Force the filling through a fine-mesh sieve into a large bowl, then add in the chocolate and butter. Let sit for 2 minutes without stirring, then whisk to combine. Whisk in the vanilla. Wrap the bowl with plastic wrap touching the surface of the mixture and refrigerate to cool completely, about 2 hours.

» Spoon the filling into the crust. Depending on the size of your crust, you may have a bit of leftover filling, but I'm sure no one will mind polishing off the last little bit! Loosely cover and refrigerate for at least 6 hours to allow the filling to set.

» Make the meringue just before you're ready to serve. Fold the remaining 2 tablespoons malt powder into the meringue, then pipe or spread it over the top of the pie. Brown the meringue lightly with a kitchen torch if desired.

½ cup sugar

¼ cup cornstarch

½ teaspoon salt

4 egg yolks

3 cups whole milk

½ cup plus 2 tablespoons barley malt extract powder or malt powder (such as Ovaltine), divided

7 ounces fine-quality bittersweet chocolate, melted

2 tablespoons unsalted butter, softened

1 teaspoon vanilla extract

1 premade 9-inch chocolate cookie piecrust

Italian Meringue (page 18)

baked eggs with honey and cinnamon

If you've ever had your custard sadly turn into scrambled eggs, you'll appreciate these baked eggs—they have that same custard flavor, but skip the tricky temperature monitoring and let the eggs just be eggs.

Makes 4 servings

¼ teaspoon ground cinnamon

¼ teaspoon freshly grated nutmeg

¼ teaspoon ground allspice

¼ teaspoon salt

4 eggs

2 tablespoons heavy cream

2 tablespoons honey, plus more for drizzling

» Preheat the oven to 400 degrees F.

» In a small bowl, mix the cinnamon, nutmeg, allspice, and salt and set aside.

» Using an immersion blender or a whisk, thoroughly blend the eggs with the cream and honey and divide the mixture among four 4-ounce ramekins. Sprinkle with the spices.

» Place the ramekins in a baking dish filled with ¼ to ½ inch of water and bake for about 10 minutes on the middle rack of your oven, until the eggs are just set. Remove the ramekins from the oven and let them cool for about a minute before serving. Drizzle with a bit more honey if desired and serve warm.

COCKTAILS

drinks that go
over easy

lime meringue margarita

Mix a margarita and a key lime pie and what do you get? Something a lot like this meringue-topped cocktail. Unlike the stiff meringues you pipe onto desserts, this meringue stays a bit softer, so it pours onto the top of the cocktail and floats in a drinkable layer.

Makes 1 cocktail

1½ ounces tequila *blanco* (aka silver tequila)

2 tablespoons freshly squeezed lime juice (from 1 medium lime)

½ ounce Cointreau

½ ounce agave nectar

1 egg white

2 teaspoons sugar

Maldon or other flaked sea salt

» Fill a cocktail shaker with ice; add the tequila, lime juice, Cointreau, and agave nectar; stir a few times until chilled. Strain into a 5-ounce stemmed glass.

» Add the egg white and sugar to a cocktail shaker with ¼ cup of ice. Shake vigorously until the egg white is fluffy.

» Pour the meringue over the back of a spoon onto the top of the margarita to help the meringue float on top of the cocktail. Garnish with a few grains of sea salt.

bumblebee cocktail

The Bumblebee is a classic sour cocktail, but it is sweetened with honey instead of sugar. If you prefer, you can use agave nectar, which pours and blends a bit easier than honey.

Makes 1 cocktail

» Add the rum, lime juice, and honey to a cocktail shaker and stir until the honey dissolves. Add ½ cup ice and shake a few times, then strain into a 5-ounce stemmed glass.

» Add the egg white and sugar to the cocktail shaker with ¼ cup of ice. Shake vigorously until the egg white is fluffy.

» Pour the meringue over the back of a spoon onto the top of the cocktail. Garnish with an orange twist.

2 ounces dark rum

2 tablespoons freshly squeezed lime juice (from one medium lime)

1½ to 2 teaspoons honey or agave nectar

2 teaspoons sugar

1 egg white

Orange peel, for garnish

From left to right: Lime Meringue Margarita, Coffee Cocktail, Bumblebee Cocktail, Navan Flip, St-Germain Fizz, Pisco Sour

navan flip

A flip is a cocktail that uses a whole egg instead of just the egg white, so you can pretend like you're Rocky while you're getting your drink on. If a whole egg skeeves you out, you can use an egg white instead, but your cocktail will be more frothy than creamy. If you can't find Navan, you can substitute another vanilla liquor, or make your own vanilla cognac by tossing a couple of whole vanilla beans into the bottle and letting it sit for a couple of weeks. You'll need to add 1 ounce of simple syrup to the cocktail for a similar flavor.

Makes 1 cocktail

2 ounces Navan vanilla cognac

2 tablespoons freshly squeezed lemon juice, (from 1 medium lemon)

1 egg

2 drops Vanilla or Angostura bitters

» Combine all ingredients except the bitters in a cocktail shaker with about ½ cup ice and shake vigorously. Strain into a 5-ounce stemmed glass and dot with bitters.

pisco sour

The pisco sour is my favorite classic cocktail. It's the perfect combination of sour and sweet, with the egg white both tempering the alcohol and giving it a lovely, light frothiness.

Makes 1 cocktail

2 ounces pisco

1 tablespoon sugar

1 tablespoon freshly squeezed lime or lemon juice

1 teaspoon egg whites

2 drops Angostura bitters

» Combine all ingredients except the bitters in a cocktail shaker with about ½ cup of ice and shake vigorously. Strain into a 5-ounce stemmed glass and dot with bitters.

st-germain fizz

A fizz is a type of classic sour cocktail that pairs sweet and sour mixers, an egg white for foam, and club soda for effervescence. This fizz adds a bit of floral and fruit for a beautiful and tasty tipple.

Makes 1 cocktail

» Combine all ingredients (except the club soda and garnish) in a cocktail shaker with about ½ cup of ice and shake vigorously. Strain into a 5-ounce stemmed glass and top with the club soda. Garnish with a fresh blackberry.

2 ounces vodka	1 egg white
1½ ounces St-Germain elderflower liqueur	Pinch of salt
	1 teaspoon sugar
2 blackberries, muddled	1 ounce club soda
2 tablespoons freshly squeezed lemon juice (from 1 medium lemon)	Blackberries for garnish

coffee cocktail

The classic coffee cocktail doesn't contain any coffee, but it looks so much like a hot cup of joe, complete with a layer of *crema*, that the name still fits.

Makes 1 cocktail

» Combine all ingredients except the nutmeg in a cocktail shaker with about ½ cup of ice and shake vigorously. Strain into a 5-ounce stemmed glass and garnish with the nutmeg.

1½ ounce cognac	1 teaspoon sugar
1½ ounce ruby port	Freshly grated nutmeg
1 egg	

INDEX

Note: Photographs are indicated by *italics*.

ABOUT THE AUTHOR

LARA FERRONI is a food geek who can't quite decide what she'd rather do: write about, style, or photograph food. But, as long as she gets to eat it in the end, she stays pretty happy. Lara is author of two cookbooks, *Doughnuts: Simple and Delicious Recipes to Make at Home* and *Real Snacks: Make Your Favorite Childhood Treats Without all the Junk*, and a photography book, *Food Photography: Pro Secrets for Styling, Lighting & Shooting*. She shoots regularly for Epicurious.com, Gourmet Live, and *Imbibe* magazine, among others. You can see more of Lara's work on her blog, LaraFerroni.com.